"It is my privilege and honor to comment on *Just Cutting It Straight 2*. This book is an excellent resource for anyone seeking Biblical interpretation to the New Testament. The hermeneutical and homiletical arrangements are superior. The concepts are outstanding. Dr. Stubblefield's gift for preaching is clearly documented in these outlines that provide major understanding and teaching for any student preaching the Bible and addressing social crisis. It is also an excellent support reading and reference for those who are involved in personal and community enhancement and empowerment. What a wonderful addition to anyone's library. I am blessed to be able to know this author and call him my friend and mentor."

Rev. Dr. Bishop E. Carter, III
Pastor, Bethsaida Baptist Church, Lexington, Kentucky
Director & Faculty Member, Simmons College of Kentucky
Chief Chaplain, (Retired) Kentucky Department of Corrections
Chaplain, 5th District, Omega Psi Phi Fraternity, Inc.

"As Luke in his second volume, the book of Acts, wrote to continue expounding on the mighty works and words of Christ by the Spirit through the ministry of the apostles, so in volume two of *Just Cutting It Straight*, Dr. T. D. Stubblefield engages the whole counsel of God in these preaching and teaching outlines from the New Testament. This volume will assist preachers in turning the ink of their biblical studies into the blood of their sermon organization."

Dr. Robert Smith, Jr.
Charles T. Carter Baptist Chair of Divinity
Beeson Divinity School
Samford University, Birmingham, Alabama

"In 1994, being a young pastor in the ministry, I was invited by Dr. Stubblefield to preach a revival at the First Baptist Church, Georgetown, Kentucky. Little did I know, I would be meeting a servant of God who would become this preacher's mentor, friend and brother beloved. Since our first encounter, I have found him to be a man after God's own heart and truly devoted to the cause of Christ. When it comes to rightly dividing the Word of Truth, he knows how to "Cut It Straight."

Dr. Stubblefield is a seasoned veteran when it comes to pastoral work. Years of study and biblical knowledge are saturated throughout the book. Having over thirty-five years of pastoral experience, he has a unique way of combining a Greek word study along with an exegetical approach of understanding selected passages of scripture. He uses his homiletical skills to expose new insights to the Word of God.

In *Just Cutting It Straight 2*, Dr. Stubblefield develops detailed sermon outlines to aid in sermon preparation just as a skillful tentmaker. With a straightedge ruler in one hand and a cutting instrument in the other, he demonstrates a pattern of how to dissect the scripture and then construct the sermon. The straighter the cut, the easier it is to connect the pieces.

Just Cutting It Straight 2 takes a deeper look into the hidden treasures of God's Word. The pages of this book are filled with precious stones that are profitable for the novice as well as any distinguished pastor, preacher or teacher. I would highly recommend this book as a good reference tool to be included in anyone's ecclesiastical library."

Rev. Dr. M. O. Fort
Senior Pastor, Virginia Street Baptist Church, Hopkinsville, Kentucky
President, Hopkinsville College of the Bible, Hopkinsville, Kentucky

----

Just Cutting It Straight 2

OUTLINES FOR PREACHING
AND TEACHING FROM THE
NEW TESTAMENT

T. D. Stubblefield

Just Cutting It Straight 2
Copyright © 2017 T. D. Stubblefield Ministries, L.L.C.

ISBN - 978-0-692-90098-7

Library of Congress Control Number: 2016902528

All Scripture quotations, unless otherwise indicated, are taken from the Holy Bible, King James Version.

Scripture quotations marked NIV are taken from the Holy Bible, New International Version. © 1973, 1978, 1984, 2011.

Scripture quotations marked MSG are taken from The Message by Eugene Peterson. © 1993, 1994, 1995, 1996, 2000, 2001, 2002.

Cover Design by Brandy Jackson

Printed in the United States by
Mira Digital Publishing
Chesterfield, Missouri 63005

CONTENTS

New Testament Outlines

ACKNOWLEDGEMENTS

I am deeply moved by the opportunity the Lord has given me to share the fruits of my biblical explorations with a wider audience. The outlines in this volume combined with those in its predecessor bring the total number of outlines to one-hundred seventy. This number is not arbitrary but is a salute to the storied historical legacy and growing missional impact of the congregation that the Lord has allowed me to serve since February 2000, and which in November 2016 celebrated one hundred seventy years of ministry in the St. Louis region. The completion of the initial manuscript of this volume in the same year is my tribute to the First Baptist Church of Chesterfield, Missouri that still serves as the vocational and experiential womb where this preacher-pastor's sermonic gifts are birthed, bent and blended for ministry to congregation, community and culture.

Once again, Dr. Kimberly Hodge-Bell (Project Manager), Brandy Jackson (Graphic Designer) and Monique Smith (Editor) have creatively and capably corroborated with me on another literary project. I am very grateful to Deidra Scott-Elbert who provided a much-needed set of eyes and ears during the initial stage of the manuscript development. I must also acknowledge the encouragement, insight and faithful stewardship of Reverend Christopher Rogers (Assistant Pastor), my spiritual son whose presence, partnership and participation in ministry with me has been of inestimable value.

Most of all, I thank God for my loving wife Judy, the mother of our four children and the matriarch of our family who has journeyed through life and ministry with me for over forty years. Her words, her walk and her wisdom inspire me still to be the best God has called me to be.

INTRODUCTION

A conference participant and young preacher said to me, *"Pastor Stubblefield, I sure would like some more of those sermon bones."* I had just completed a workshop on expository preaching which he had attended. I distributed notes and some samples of my sermon outlines to the attendees. His request, while framed in some crude and ambiguous vernacular was not facetious, foolish or frivolous, but a sincere commendation of the skeletal outlines in the handout. I encouraged each preacher and pastor in attendance that day to add their own flesh to the bones I had provided.

This experience took place over twenty-five years ago and still haunts me in a helpful way. It, as much as anything else I've experienced in life and in ministry, has birthed within me an inextinguishable stewardship that eventuated in the publication last year of the first volume of the <u>Just Cutting It Straight</u> series of preaching and teaching outlines.

Like its predecessor, this volume is an archaeological dig of sorts. With great care, prayer and intentionality, as a Pastor-Teacher and Preacher for the past thirty-four and forty years respectively, I have sought to exhume, examine and evaluate the fossilized but still vital, vibrant, vigorous and valuable remains of key biblical passages and process my findings primarily for the two historic congregations God called me to serve. For the greater part of this journey, I did not anticipate that this labor of love would someday be shared with the larger Body of Christ.

This volume of <u>Just Cutting It Straight</u> is an attempt to provide "some more" of those sermon bones. It focuses on the New Testament Books. Very early in my ministry, a wise pastor, mentor and lover of God's Word shared with me that the "Old Testament is the New Testament revealed and the New Testament is the Old Testament fulfilled." My embrace and endorsement of this fundamental hermeneutical axiom has not waned or wavered over the years. The outlines that comprise these pages implicitly and explicitly pay homage to this irrefutable claim.

Bathed in the intimate correlation, compassion, cooperation and community that occurs uniquely in the spiritual relationship between Pastor, People and Paraclete, these outlines while anchored in biblical passages that date back to antiquity, speak with a renewing relevance to the contemporary life of the child of God where faith, hope and love must be exposed, experienced and expressed. These outlines anchored sermons that aimed to address the strengths and the struggles of God's people.

Like the epic narrative of the prophet Ezekiel, let down in the midst of a valley full of dry bones, I too have been humbled and haunted by the timeless interrogation by the Master of the Messenger, "Can these bones live?" As Ezekiel understood, the answer and the truth rest solely and ultimately in God's knowledge and power. I can only say that these outlines represent my experience of the activity of the life-giving God who has time and time again breathed on my pastoral, ministerial and sermonic bones, bringing them to life, and letting them "stand on their feet, an exceeding mighty army" (Ezekiel 37:10).

I pray this volume of "bones" will encourage you to appreciate their march, listen to their cadence and believe that God can animate your service, situation and sermons by His Grace and for His Glory! By inference and admission, these skeletal submissions are by nature naked and bare and in need of the supernatural covering that develops in the sacred union of Word and Witness. To that end, I have incorporated many of the features of the first volume. To conserve space, when particular passages are cited, the larger biblical context is bracketed. Introductory remarks, illustrations and other supporting material have been added to encourage clarity, continuity and creativity.

As always, the alliteration is secondary to the textual development and reflective only of the unique spiritual signature God has given me. Also, in this volume, I have added eschatological trajectories to a number of the outlines. Effective biblical preaching and teaching always extend and expand the horizons of our hope in Christ. My mentor, dear friend and beloved spiritual brother, Dr. Robert Smith, Jr., call these textual tonalities *"sermonic eschatonics."* They reflect the celebrative and anticipatory note so uniquely resonant in the African-American pulpit.

The textual coordinates or context is provided in most of the outlines so readers can identify the specific biblical address from which each movement or point in the outline is derived from the vast galaxy of the Scriptures. In other outlines, the reader is encouraged to consider the larger context of the passage or consider applications. In some instances, I willfully dialed back the volume of information I could have provided for a particular outline or point in order to create a *textual teaser* that encourages the reader's own reflection and reconnaissance. When facing the "Goliaths" in ministry and in life, we must be careful not to put on Saul's armor. The fit can be fatal. Every communicator of the Word of God while leveraging the rich resources of generations of preachers, pastors and teachers must also be careful to cultivate their own unique style and voice. This is what makes the Gospel a never-ending story!

NEW TESTAMENT OUTLINES

– 1 –

The Missing Star
(An Advent Message)

Matthew 2:1-2 [1-12] (KJV)

¹ Now when Jesus was born in Bethlehem of Judaea in the days of Herod the king, behold, there came wise men from the east to Jerusalem, ² Saying, Where is he that is born King of the Jews? for we have seen his star in the east, and are come to worship him.

In Hollywood, California tourists visit the legendary Walk of the Stars. Cinematic success and movie stardom determines who's in and who's out. A handprint on the sidewalk literally cements an actor's star status. Someone once said, "Stir a flower and you trouble a star." In this text, wise men from the East stirred the passion of their curiosity and concern and became timeless authenticators of the birth of the Messiah.

Much too often however, Jesus rather than being the "Bright and Morning Star" of our existence and experience becomes the "Missing Star."

I.   The Missing Star in Our Witness (verses 1-7)

II. The Missing Star in Our Work (verses 8-10)

III. The Missing Star in Our Worship (verses 11-12)

    a. The business of these wise men was worship

        i.   They left home

        ii. They inquired

        iii. They were prepared

        iv. They brought gifts

        v.   They went home another way

"Star of wonder, star of night,
Star with loyal beauty bright,
Westward leading, still proceeding,
Guide us into thy perfect light."

– 2 –

Moving from Huddle to Harvest

Matthew 9:35-38 (KJV)

[35] And Jesus went about all the cities and villages, teaching in their synagogues, and preaching the gospel of the kingdom, and healing every sickness and every disease among the people. [36] But when he saw the multitudes, he was moved with compassion on them, because they fainted, and were scattered abroad, as sheep having no shepherd. [37] Then saith he unto his disciples, The harvest truly *is* plenteous, but the labourers *are* few; [38] Pray ye therefore the Lord of the harvest, that he will send forth labourers into his harvest.

Anyone who has ever watched a football game knows that when the offense takes the field, their primary goal is to advance the ball against the opposing team's defense. As they begin their offensive series, the offense huddles together behind the line of scrimmage as the quarterback calls the play. Usually, the play is designed by the coach who is the offensive coordinator. At the end of the huddle, the offense breaks and moves to the line of scrimmage and executes the play. If the offense takes too long to execute the play, the referee will call delay of game and assess a penalty that will take the team in the opposite and wrong direction.

When Jesus shares these words with His disciples, the Jewish religion had become one massive huddle. The Temple was teeming with worshippers on the Sabbath; there was a synagogue in every hamlet and village, six thousand Pharisees and Sadducees served in positions of ecclesiastical authority, and approximately twenty thousand priests and Levites ministered daily in the Temple. But someone had forgotten to say "break" and the team never left the huddle to execute the play that would advance the Kingdom of God.

I.   Model the Master (verse 35a)

a. His ministry was (verse 35b)

    i. mobile

    ii. meaningful

    iii. momentous

II. Mobilize the Mission (verses 36 - 37)

III. Marshall the Might (verse 38)

> *"I want Jesus to walk with me,*
> *I want Jesus to walk with me,*
> *I want Jesus to walk with me,*
> *All along my pilgrim journey,*
> *I want Jesus to walk with me."* (Negro Spiritual)

– 3 –

The Magnificent Merger

Matthew 11:28-30 (KJV)

²⁸ **Come unto me, all** *ye* **that labour and are heavy laden,
and I will give you rest.**
²⁹ **Take my yoke upon you, and learn of me; for I am meek and
lowly in heart: and ye shall find rest unto your souls.**
³⁰ **For my yoke** *is* **easy, and my burden is light.**

In modern times, corporate mergers are fairly common as far as business practices go. They are so commonplace that even persons not schooled in the basic principles or vagaries of economics understand what a merger is. The reality is that businesses of one size or another join forces every day of the week, due to the increased efficiency or market share such arrangements or partnerships offer. Not all mergers are so casual or common. Some could be described as seismic, involving companies so large that simply by merging, they send shock waves throughout the economy, and affect tidal-like changes in the way business is done within entire industries. These mergers involve billions of dollars, thousands of employees and untold amounts of intellectual property changing hands.

According to the dictionary, the word "merger" means "to absorb" or "combine" or even "to swallow up" or "sink." That being the case, the most magnificent merger of all is recorded in this biblical passage and its larger context in this chapter, the Gospel of Matthew and the canonical Scriptures.

I.   The Person that Commends It *("Come unto **me**")*

II. The Problem that Compels It *("All ye **that labour** and **are heavy laden**")*

III. The Promise that Confirms It *("And I will give you **rest**")*

> *"That word above all earthly powers*
> *No thanks to them abideth,*
> *The Spirit and the gifts are ours*
> *Thru Him who with us sideth."* (Martin Luther)

– 4 –

Keyed for Victory

Matthew 16:18 [13-20] (KJV)

[18] And I say also unto thee, That thou art Peter, and upon this rock I will build my church; and the gates of hell shall not prevail against it.

A few years ago while preaching in the Washington D.C. area, I shared an elevator with a man who seemed quite annoyed. He had checked in at the hotel where we both were staying, gone to his room on an upper floor with quite a bit of luggage in tow only to discover that his key did not work. Repeated swipes had failed to open the door. I thought then and I do now that this man's experience was endemic of life. So much of our failure, frustration and futility in life and in the church are related to the fact that we are using the wrong key or the key doesn't work.

It occurred to me that Jesus was signaling just the opposite in this passage. At this point in his ministry, Jesus is intensifying the preparation of His disciples; the Cross is looming before Him and there, amidst the rocky knolls of Caesarea Philippi and against the backdrop of the mighty and majestic summit of Mount Hermon, Jesus promises the disciples the keys to the kingdom. This text is a timeless reminder that the church is keyed for victory.

I.   Keyed with the Faith in a Supernatural Revelation (verses 13 – 17)

II. Keyed with the Foundation of a Supernatural Redemption (verse 18a)

III. Keyed with the Force of a Supernatural Resistance (verse 18b)

IV. Keyed with the Function of a Supernatural Resourcefulness (verses 19 – 20)

    a. Possession of a key represents position, power, privilege, pedigree and provision

"I heard an old story,
How a Savior came from glory,
How He gave His live on Calvary
To save a wretch like me;
I heard about His groaning,
Of His precious blood's atoning,
Then I repented of my sins and won the victory."

(Eugene M. Bartlett)

– 5 –

When the Lord Handles Our Business

Matthew 17:24-27 (NIV)

[24] After Jesus and his disciples arrived in Capernaum, the collectors of the two-drachma tax came to Peter and asked, "Doesn't your teacher pay the temple tax?"
[25] "Yes, he does," he replied. When Peter came into the house, Jesus was the first to speak. "What do you think, Simon?" he asked. "From whom do the kings of the earth collect duty and taxes--from their own sons or from others?" [26] "From others," Peter answered. "Then the sons are exempt," Jesus said to him. [27] "But so that we may not offend them, go to the lake

and throw out your line. Take the first fish you catch; open its mouth and you will find a four-drachma coin. Take it and give it to them for my tax and yours."

There is no part of our lives that Jesus is not interested in. He is a faithful High Priest who understands all that we are going through (Hebrews 4:15). He covers our entrances and our exits in life with His presence, power and provision (Psalm 121). The newspaper reported a deadly accident a few years ago with the headline that said, *"Crashes follow a deadly pattern .... . A driver not paying attention ..."* This text reminds us that God pays attention to us.

    I.   A Responsibility We Engage (verses 24 -25a)

    II.   A Relationship We Enjoy (verses 25b – 26)

    III. A Resource We Employ (verse 27)

    IV. A Redemption We Embrace (*context and application*)

        a.   A prolepsis (preview) of the Gospel in this text. What was the mission of Jesus on this planet? **Another bill had come due.** That bill was paid on Calvary. Archaeologists have found scrawled on tax receipts used during this period the word *tetetelestai* which means "it is finished" or "paid in full." These are the very words Jesus uttered from the Cross before He dismissed His spirit.

– 6 –

Go Farther

Matthew 26:39 [36-45] (KJV)

[39] **And he went a little further, and fell on his face, and prayed, saying, O my Father, if it be possible, let this cup pass from me: nevertheless not as I will, but as thou *wilt*.**

This passage records the riveting account of Jesus agonizing in prayer in the Garden of Gethsemane. This text and its parallels in Mark 14:35 (*"went forward"*) and Luke 22:41 (*"withdrew from them"*) emphasize the dual themes of separation and animation that were so characteristic of the ministry of Jesus. His attitude and actions here constitute a challenge to every believer and to every local church. The late Bishop Fulton Sheen once said that in the church "there are too many come comes and not enough go go's." Jesus demonstrated three commitments when He went a little further.

I.   A Commitment to His Father's Person (*"my Father"*)

II. A Commitment to His Father's Plan (*"let this cup pass from me"*)

III. A Commitment to His Father's People (*context and application*)

"What can wash away my sin?
Nothing but the blood of Jesus
What can make me whole again?
Nothing but the blood of Jesus.

O precious is the flow
That makes me white as snow
None other fount I know,
Nothing but the blood of Jesus." (Robert Lowry)

– 7 –

No Parking

Matthew 28:18-20 (KJV)

[18] And Jesus came and spake unto them, saying, All power is given unto me in heaven and in earth. [19] Go ye therefore, and teach all nations, baptizing them in the name of the Father, and of the Son, and of the Holy Ghost: [20] Teaching them to observe all things whatsoever I have commanded you: and, lo, I am with you alway, *even* unto the end of the world. Amen.

Motorists know that there are designated areas where parking is either restricted or not permitted at all. This very familiar text is forever a moving and momentous reminder that God has placed a NO PARKING sign in the very interior and heart of the church's ministry. It is commonly known as the Great Commission. The verses that constitute this commission occur only here in the Gospel of Matthew which is a scorching critique of Judaism which had double parked within the corridors and confines of encrusted tradition. Jesus rebuked them for "making the Word of God of no effect because of the traditions handed down from the fathers" (Mark 7:13). Jesus condemned their crippling narrowness and the "we've never done it that way before" mentality.

These verses are relevant to the church today. There is always the temptation to move in rather than move out or to settle on the premises rather than stand on the promises (Acts 3). Consequently, the Great Commission has become in many instances the "great omission" as churches become more stationary than missionary.

I.   The Commissioning Authority Says No Parking ("*And Jesus said*")

II. The Compelling Agenda Says No Parking ("*Go ye therefore and teach all nations* ")

III. The Comprehensive Arena Says No Parking ("*baptizing them … teaching them*")

IV. The Comforting Assurance Says No Parking (*And lo, I am with you alway*")

> *"How to reach the masses, men of every birth,*
> *For an answer Jesus gave the key.*
> *And I, if I be lifted up from the earth,*
> *Will draw all men unto Me."* (Johnson Oatman, Jr.)

When Jesus is in the House

Mark 2:1-5 (NIV)

[1] A few days later, when Jesus again entered Capernaum, the people heard that he had come home. [2] So many gathered that there was no room left, not even outside the door, and he preached the word to them. [3] Some men came, bringing to him a paralytic, carried by four of them. [4] Since they could not get him to Jesus because of the crowd, they made an opening in the roof above Jesus and, after digging through it, lowered the mat the paralyzed man was lying on. [5] When Jesus saw their faith, he said to the paralytic, "Son, your sins are forgiven."

Early in the public ministry of Jesus, the Gospel writer Mark records that Jesus "was in the house." Capernaum was the base of His Galilean ministry. It was also the site of a large Jewish synagogue. Crowds converged upon the scene and witnessed to the chagrin of the religious leaders, one of the notable miracles that distinguished Jesus as Israel's true Priest, Prophet and King. There are some things that happen when Jesus is in the house.

I.   Contagious Communication

      a.   It was "noised"

      b.   When it comes to Jesus, the church should be a "rumor-mill" in a positive sense.

II.   Curious Congregating

      a.   The crowd that gathered around Jesus was a curious mixture

          i.   Shallow spectators

          ii.   Self-serving opportunists

          iii. Religious hypocrites

          iv. The sinful, sick and suffering

III. Compelling Cooperation

      a.   Four friends, each carrying a corner bring their friend to Jesus

i. A provocative portrait of authentic ministry

IV. Costly Consecration

    a. **Who paid for the roof?**

– 9 –

When Jesus Comes to Church

Mark 3:1-5 (KJV)

[1] **And he entered again into the synagogue; and there was a man there which had a withered hand. [2] And they watched him, whether he would heal him on the sabbath day; that they might accuse him. [3] And he saith unto the man which had the withered hand, Stand forth. [4] And he saith unto them, Is it lawful to do good on the sabbath days, or to do evil? to save life, or to kill? But they held their peace. [5] And when he had looked round about on them with anger, being grieved for the hardness of their hearts, he saith unto the man, Stretch forth thine hand. And he stretched *it* out: and his hand was restored whole as the other.**

The church is a place where no one is too good to stay out and no one is too bad to come in. Jesus meets us at our point of need. This is the essence of the Incarnation for, as Eugene Peterson states it so profoundly in The Message, "The Word became flesh and blood, and moved into the neighborhood" (John 1:14a). While the immediate context of this text is a synagogue in Capernaum of Galilee, Jesus still visits His people whenever and wherever we gather. When He does, there is:

I. Purposeful Sovereignty (*"And he entered again into the synagogue"*)

II. Painful Suffering (*"There was a man there with had a withered hand"*)

III. Proud Superiority (*"And they watched him, whether he would heal him on the Sabbath day; that they might accuse him."*)

IV. Proven Sufficiency (*"Stretch forth thine hand"*)

Taking Back Stolen Property

Mark 3:27 [22-30] (KJV)

**27 No man can enter into a strong man's house,
and spoil his goods, except he will first bind the strong man;
and then he will spoil his house.**

Two-thirds of the Gospel of Mark focuses on the passion of Christ. Mark accentuates the adversarial nature of the Lord's redemptive mission to a primarily Gentile audience. Jesus conquers and subjugates His enemies and according to Hebrews 10:12-13, "But this man, after he had offered one sacrifice for sins for ever, sat down on the right hand of God; From henceforth expecting till his enemies be made his footstool." His victory is strategic and not just tactical. His decisive action restores order to a broken universe and to our broken lives.

I.   The Criticism He Endured (verse 22 – 26)

II. The Conflict He Engaged (verse 27)

    a.   He bent

    b.   He bore

    c.   He broke (through the threshold of the enemy)

III. The Confidence He Encourages (verses 28 – 30)

    a.   We are dividing the spoils of a victory

"Therefore I'll reward him extravagantly – the best of everything, the highest honors – Because he looked death in the face and didn't flinch, because he embraced the company of the lowest. He took on his own shoulders the sin of the many, he took up the cause of all the black sheep." (Isaiah 53:12 - <u>The Message Bible</u>)

A Traveler's Advisory

Mark 4:39 [35-41] (KJV)

[39] And he arose, and rebuked the wind, and said unto the sea,
Peace, be still. And the wind ceased,
and there was a great calm.

The great hymnist, William Cowper penned these immortal words, "God works in mysterious ways; His wonders to perform. He plants His footsteps in the sea and rides on every storm." The Psalmist shares a similar sentiment when he writes, "He maketh the storm a calm, so that the waves thereof are still" (Psalm 107:29 KJV).

At this point in the Gospel of Mark, Jesus has already demonstrated His power over disease and the demonic. Now, He establishes His dominance over nature. Whatever He tells us to do, we should be confident even in the midst of inclement spiritual weather that He is in control.

I. The Unavoidable Demand (verses 35 – 36)

II. The Urgent Danger (verse 37)

III. The Unsettling Doubt (verse 38)

    a. *"The mind is quick to turn from simple faith to the cant and fury of fools who never learn. Reason embraces death; while out of frightening eyes still stirs the wish to love."* (Theodore Roethke)

IV. The Unprecedented Deliverance (verse 39)

    a. Sometimes He calms the storm within us before calming the storm around us.

V. The Unceasing Declaration (verses 40 – 41)

    a. "What manner of man is this?" It is a rhetorical question to which the rest of the Gospel provides the answer.

"God works in a mysterious way
His wonders to perform;
He plants his footsteps in the sea,
He rides upon the storm." (William Cowper)

– 12 –

Don't Go Home Without It!

Mark 5:19-20 [1-20] (KJV)

[19] Howbeit Jesus suffered him not, but saith unto him, Go home to thy friends, and tell them how great things the Lord hath done for thee, and hath had compassion on thee. [20] And he departed, and began to publish in Decapolis how great things Jesus had done for him: and all *men* did marvel.

In the 1970's the American Express Company began promoting its traveler's checks and credit cards with the slogan, "Don't leave home without it!" This popular promotional slogan was revived in 2005.

The man in our text, who had been tragically separated from family and friends, was ordered to "go home." This is the only occurrence of the phrase "go home" in the New Testament. It deserves close attention. Jesus clearly demonstrated in this text that not only is He concerned about what happens when we leave home but more importantly what occurs when we go home. Whatever else we do in the life of the church, we must strengthen the family; we should make sure that we encourage the resolve of those who must GO HOME.

I. The Crisis that Crippled Him (verses 1 – 5)

II. The Concern that Compelled Him (verses 6 – 13)

    a. He begged the Lord that he might be with Him!

III. The Commission that Challenged Him (verses 14 – 20)

    a. Not the ecclesiastical commission of Mark 16:15

    b. Not the apostolic commission of Mark 6:7

    c.   But the home and family commission which is perhaps the most difficult and daunting of all

IV. The Christ that Cured Him (*application*)

– 13 –

Issues and Answers

Mark 5:34 [25 – 34] (NIV)

³⁴ **He said to her, "Daughter, your faith has healed you. Go in peace and be freed from your suffering."**

The healing of the woman with the issue of blood is recorded in all the Synoptic Gospels. The repetition, redundancy and reiteration are not without purpose. This woman had exhausted all of her resources trying to get well. In quiet desperation, she felt the fabric of His garment and knew something had profoundly changed with her condition. He was the answer to her issue.

I.   The Condition that Afflicted Her (verse 25)

II.   The Cure that Avoided Her (verse 26)

III. The Christ that Attracted Her (verse 27)

IV. The Confidence that Assured Her (verse 28 – 29)

V.   The Connection that Anchored Her (verses 30 – 34)

    a.   "Daughter" addressed her disease and more importantly, her disconnection. No longer shrouded in anonymity, she was now a member of the Royal Family!

Why Settle for the Crumbs
When You Can Have the Crust?

Mark 7:28 [24-30] (KJV)

[28] And she answered and said unto him, Yes, Lord: yet the dogs under the table eat of the children's crumbs.

Jesus was weary and worn out from the growing strain of ministry. He needed time for rest and renewal. He withdrew to this region but the Bible says, *"He could not be hid"* (Mark 7:24b). And He could not and would not be hid from this "certain woman" in our text who refused to settle for the crumbs of her dire and depleted circumstances; she wanted the crust of dignity and distinction from the Lord for her daughter and for herself. She would not resign herself to second class citizenship. But what did she do? What does the text tell us?

I.   She Sought the Master (verse 24 – 25)

II. She Seized the Moment (verses 26 – 28)

III. She Secured the Message (verses 29 – 30)

   a. So real was the truth that the Master had shared with her that she began acting like it was a reality. This is what authentic faith does!

IV. She Saw the Miracle ("And **when she was come to her house,** she found the devil gone out, and her daughter laid upon her bed")

   a. It was only when "she got home" that she found her daughter was healed.

   b. What happens when we get **home?**

"I've got a new home, over in glory,
And it's mine, mine, mine!
I've got a new home, over in glory,
And it's mine, mine, mine." (Negro Spiritual)

A Crisis of Faith

Mark 9:23-24 [14-29] (KJV)

[23] Jesus said unto him, If thou canst believe, all things *are* possible to him that believeth. [24] And straightway the father of the child cried out, and said with tears, Lord, I believe; help thou mine unbelief.

The story of the father and his epileptic son is recorded in Matthew, Mark and Luke. The account in Mark is the most complete and comprehensive owing most likely to Mark's dependence on Peter's eyewitness account. The focus in this passage is on faith. This text reminds us that faith is not always standing strong and erect on the promenade of life, ready, willing and able to spread its wings and take eternity into its grasp. More often than we would like, our faith is in crisis anxiously groping in the dark and dense mazes of life trying to make sense of our circumstances and clawing its way sometimes reluctantly to the Light.

Each participant and player in the narrative embodies some aspect of a faith crisis. The father's crisis of belief is unwilling; the son's uncontrollable; the disciples' unconscious and the Jewish scribes' mocking and willful. When the story is concluded, the father is comforted, the son is cured, the disciples empowered and the scribes silenced and rebuked.

I.   Roots of a Faith Crisis (verses 17 – 18)

    a.   The disciples' impotence exacerbated the crisis; is this message for the contemporary church?

II.   Resources for a Faith Crisis (verses 20 – 29)

    a.   The Supreme Object of our Faith

    b.   The Supernatural Operation of our Faith

How to Talk to a Mountain

Mark 11:22-23 [22-24] (NIV)

[22] "Have faith in God," Jesus answered. [23] "I tell you the truth, if anyone says to this mountain, 'Go, throw yourself into the sea,' and does not doubt in his heart but believes that what he says will happen, it will be done for him.

In the Scriptures, mountains are often associated with the presence, provision and protection of God. But in this passage, the mountain symbolizes the obstacles and challenges that we face in life. Christianity is lived out in the shade and shadow of mountainous terrain. Just as we have some rivers to cross and valleys to go through, we also have some mountains to climb. The Scriptures remind us that our God has a special attraction to mountains and mountainous terrain. Some of the moving moments in biblical history occurred on or in the vicinity of mountains. On these mountains, God talks to us, we talk to God and, by faith can even talk to the mountain.

I. Mountain Rhetoric (verses 22 – 23a)

II. Mountain Removal (verses 23b – 24)

III. Mountain Redemption (*context and application*)

IV. This text anticipates what will happen on "a hill far away … "

V. Mountain Rejoicing (*context and application*)

    a. What do we do when our mountains are moved?

"Have you any rivers
That seem uncrossable?
And have you any mountain
That you cannot tunnel through?

God specializes
In things thought impossible
And he will do what no other
No other power but holy power can do." (Roberta Martin)

The Anatomy of a Servant

Mark 13:34-37 (NIV)

[34] It's like a man going away: He leaves his house and puts his servants in charge, each with his assigned task, and tells the one at the door to keep watch. [35] "Therefore keep watch because you do not know when the owner of the house will come back--whether in the evening, or at midnight, or when the rooster crows, or at dawn. [36] If he comes suddenly, do not let him find you sleeping. [37] What I say to you, I say to everyone: 'Watch!'"

This text is recorded with some variation in all the Synoptic Gospels – cf. Matthew 24:36-51; Luke 21:34-36. This parable is pocketed in a larger passage that raises the prospect of the Lord's second coming and the appropriate response on the part of those who are His servants.

I.   The Warrant of a Servant *("put his servants in charge")*

II. The Work of a Servant *("each with his assigned task")*

III. The Watch of a Servant *("and tells the one at the door to keep watch")*

   a. The territory we traverse and the conflict we are in necessitate that we watch.

   b. The times and seasons in which we live necessitate that we watch.

   c. The imminent return of our Lord and Savior Jesus Christ necessitates that we watch.

IV. The Worth (Wealth) of a Servant *("do not let him find you")*

   a. Implicit in this text is the valuation of the servant in the eye and estimation of the Master.

"He is no fool who gives up what he cannot keep to gain what he cannot lose." (Dr. Martin Luther King, Jr.)

Living Life in the Affirmative
(An Advent Message)

Luke 1:38 [26-38] (KJV)

[38] And Mary said, Behold the handmaid of the Lord; be it unto me according to thy word. And the angel departed from her.

Mary, the virgin mother of Jesus holds a place of honor among the women of the New Testament. As the first member of the human race to accept Christ, she stands at the apex of Christian history as an enduring model of faith, humility and service. She speaks seven times in the Gospels and then is silent. She is not the mother of grace but a model of grace. While her first words recorded in this text express doubt; her last words mirror the dignity and deference of a woman with great faith in God. Mary was a woman, a wife and mother who lived her life in the affirmative.

I.   Saying Yes to the Expression of God's Remarkable Purposes (verses 26 – 30)

II. Saying Yes to the Experience of God's Radical Reproductive Power (verses 31 – 32)

III. Saying Yes to Exaltation of God's Redeeming Provision and Pardon (verses 33 – 38)

    a.   This passage begins with a pronouncement and ends with praise!

"All to Jesus I surrender,
Make me Savior, wholly Thine,
Let me feel the Holy Spirit,
Truly know that Thou art mine." (Judson W. Van De Venter)

– 19 –

Our Father's Business

Luke 2:49 [41-51] (KJV)

⁴⁹ **And he said unto them, How is it that ye sought me? wist ye not that I must be about my Father's business?**

There are variations in the translation of the word "business" in verse 49. The <u>New Revised Standard Version,</u> <u>New Living Translation</u> and <u>New International Version</u> translate it "house." The <u>Young's Literal Translation</u> is "the things." Regardless, this is a passage that chronicles Jesus in His perfect humanity coming of age and developing a growing sense of self-awareness and self-identity. Even at the age of twelve years old, He was focused on His Father's business.

I.   The Ownership of the Business (*"my Father's business"*)

II.   The Operation of the Business (*context and application*)

III.   The Obligation of the Business (*context and application*)

    a. He settled in the house of God

    b. He sought the truth of God

    c. He submitted to the laws of God

IV.   The Outlook of the Business (*context and application*)

    a. The church has a responsibility to share with the world this unique "business opportunity." We are not ultimately concerned with profit but with pardon.

    b. The church exclusively has an incredible public offering (IPO) to make to a broken and sinful world.

From Mother to Son
(A Mother's Day Message)

Luke 7:14-15 [11 – 17] (NIV)

¹⁴ Then he went up and touched the coffin, and those carrying
it stood still. He said, "Young man, I say to you, get up!"
¹⁵ The dead man sat up and began to talk,
and Jesus gave him back to his mother.

This is one of three distinct miracles in the Gospels where
Jesus resuscitated someone back from the dead. I've imagined
a conversation between this widowed mother and her only son
later during the day; when the excitement had died down and
the crowds had scattered; when she and her son were home
alone and the mother began to tell her son about Jesus and what
happened that day.

That type of conversation is so reflective and representative of
what mothers do. It is one reason why we love them and respect
them; all of us have been the bountiful beneficiary of our mother
or grandmother or some mother's wise counsel. Many of them
have willed by their example our faith in the LORD.

I.   Jesus will see you in your largest crowd (*"and much
people"*)

II.   Jesus will meet you in your darkest hour (*"dead man
carried out, the only son of his mother"*)

III.   Jesus will feel you in your deepest pain (*"He had
compassion on her, and said unto her, Weep not"*)

IV.   Jesus will deliver you in your greatest trial (*"And he that
was dead, sat up"*)

Women of Substance
(A Mother's Day Message)

Luke 8:1-3 (KJV)

[1] And it came to pass afterward, that he went throughout every city and village, preaching and shewing the glad tidings of the kingdom of God: and the twelve *were* with him, [2] And certain women, which had been healed of evil spirits and infirmities, Mary called Magdalene, out of whom went seven devils, [3] And Joanna the wife of Chuza Herod's steward, and Susanna, and many others, which ministered unto him of their substance.

The seventh chapter of this Gospel records how a woman's life was changed who was touched by Jesus (7:36-50) and the eighth chapter records how a woman's life was changed who touched Jesus (8:43-48). Pocketed between these textual bookends are *"women of substance,"* some significant sisters serving a satisfying Savior. This text is especially timeless and timely in light of the disconnection and disorientation in our society today around the role of women in the marriage, the family, the workplace and in even in the church.

I.   Their Common Connection (*"certain women"*)

II. Their Dynamic Deliverance (*"which had been healed"*)

    a.   One of the women identified in the text is Mary Magdalene. This gifted, intelligent, bright and charismatic woman had been plagued with seven demons. Her gifts had been hijacked, her opportunities handcuffed, and her possibilities hamstrung. But she had experienced divine and dynamic healing from her infirmity. The seven demons that plagued and pummeled her are symbolic and symptomatic of the demonic destroyers that prey on women today – depression, fear, low self-esteem, abuse, addiction, doubts, procrastination, bitterness and self-pity. Mary was a woman who had been dynamically delivered.

III. Their Meaningful Ministry (*"ministered unto him of their substance"*)

    a. Their ministry had substance because it was...

        i. Significant and not superficial

        ii. Consequential and not controversial

        iii. Private and not public

        iv. Complementary and not competitive

        v. Sacrificial and not selfish

– 22 –

Roadside Assistance

Luke 10:34-35 [30-37] (KJV)

[34] **And went to *him*, and bound up his wounds, pouring in oil and wine, and set him on his own beast, and brought him to an inn, and took care of him.**
[35] **And on the morrow when he departed, he took out two pence, and gave *them* to the host, and said unto him, Take care of him; and whatsoever thou spendest more, when I come again, I will repay thee.**

This notable parable was Jesus' response to an expert (scribe) of the Law; who came to him attempting to justify himself; when his motives were exposed, he attempted to deflate and deflect the real issues related to his own moral and spiritual life by asking a debater's question. He knew all too well that his definition of a "neighbor" was exclusive, narrow and prejudicial, so he asked the Lord, "And who is my neighbor?" Jesus does not answer his question directly but changes the whole compass and trajectory of the question from not "who is your neighbor?" but "who are you a neighbor to?" This exchange brings this parable to the big screen of the Scriptures. Some expositors argue that it is not a parable at all but based on a real event that the scribe knew all too well. Regardless, the "good" Samaritan provided roadside assistance and by his actions transformed the definition of a "neighbor." We should go and do likewise.

I.   He Was Beat Up by the Messed Up (verse 30)

II.   He Was Passed Up by the Dressed Up (verses 31-32)

III. He was Helped Up by the Graced Up (verses 33-37)

– 23 –

Too Busy to Be Blessed
(Overcoming the Attraction of Distraction)

Luke 10:41-42 [38-42] (NIV)

⁴¹ "Martha, Martha," the Lord answered,
"you are worried and upset about many things,
⁴² but only one thing is needed.
Mary has chosen what is better,
and it will not be taken away from her."

This passage is unique to the Gospel of Luke. Although there is some debate around the placement of this passage in the Gospel chronologically, most expositors believe that what occurs in this passage takes place very close to the time [approximately four months] that Jesus makes His final trip to Jerusalem. Its value to us is that the text and its teaching constitute a timeless reminder about the dangerous attraction of distraction in the Christian life.

On this particular occasion, Martha was too busy to be blessed. On the other hand, every time we meet Mary in the Gospels, she occupies the same position; she is sitting near the feet of Jesus. Here she listened to His Word (10:39); in John 11:32, she shares her grief around the death of her brother Lazarus and in John 12:32, she anoints Jesus' feet with precious perfume and then literally "lets her hair down" and wipe them clean with her hair. What can we learn from this text?

I.   Invite Jesus In

II.   Maintain the Focus

III. Embrace the Promise

  a. Mary understood that everything else in life was just an appetizer and that Jesus was the main course. Like the woman of Samaria (John 4), she had discovered a well of water that could never run dry.

    i.   Fads will flatten

    ii.   Fashions will fail

    iii. Youth will fade

    iv. Beauty is deceitful

    v.   Favor is vain

    vi. Success is shallow

    vii. Friends will falter

    viii. Steps will shorten

    ix. Vision will weaken

    x.   Bodies will decay

  b. But God's Word will last forever … .

"I want to live so, God can use me,
Anytime Lord, anywhere!
I want to live so, God can use me,
Anytime Lord, anywhere." (Negro Spiritual)

– 24 –

It Pays to Pray

Luke 11:10 [5-10] (NIV)

[10] For everyone who asks receives; he who seeks finds; and to him who knocks, the door will be opened.

The contextual setting of this parable is Near Eastern hospitality; there were expected courtesies extended to guests who travelled at night and arrived in a village or town in need of food and shelter; no 7/11's, convenience stores or 24-hour drive throughs were available. The friend in this parable was not self-centered but "other-centered." It was "a knock at midnight" from a stranger that compelled him to go to his friend and ask for bread.

I. The Insufficiency that Evokes Our Prayers (verses 5-6)

II. The Intensity that Energizes Our Prayers (verses 7-8)

III. The Incentive that Encourages Our Prayers (verses 9-10)

    a. The conservative Jewish theologian, Joachim Jeremias gets to the heart of the principle that Jesus is expounding in this parable. Persistence on the part of the petitioner is not why it pays to pray but rather the character of God. He says,

        i. "If the friend, roused from sleep at night, hastens without a moment's delay to fulfill the request of a neighbor in difficulty, even though the whole family must be disturbed by the drawing of the bolt, how much more will God be willing to act! He hears the cry of the needy, and comes to their help. He does more than they ask. On that you may rely with all confidence."

    b. In a similar vein, the great church reformer, Martin Luther said, "Prayer is not overcoming God's reluctance but laying hold of His highest willingness."

"What a Friend, we have in Jesus,
All our sins and griefs to bear!
What a privilege to carry,
Everything to God in prayer." (Joseph Scriven)

The Biography of a Fool

Luke 12:16-21 [13 -21] (KJV)

[16] And he spake a parable unto them, saying, The ground of a certain rich man brought forth plentifully: [17] And he thought within himself, saying, What shall I do, because I have no room where to bestow my fruits? [18] And he said, This will I do: I will pull down my barns, and build greater; and there will I bestow all my fruits and my goods. [19] And I will say to my soul, Soul, thou hast much goods laid up for many years; take thine ease, eat, drink, *and* be merry. [20] But God said unto him, *Thou* fool, this night thy soul shall be required of thee: then whose shall those things be, which thou hast provided? [21] So *is* he that layeth up treasure for himself, and is not rich toward God.

Jesus addresses the subject of money in sixteen of thirty-eight parables in the Gospels. While there are five hundred verses on prayer in the four Gospels and almost five hundred on faith, there are over two thousand verses on money. This is timely in light of the human quest for the quantifiable, the relentless race for riches; the wooing of wealth, the tyranny of the temporal and the mantra of the materialistic. Jesus called the man in this parable a "fool."

I.   His Disturbing Self-Centeredness (verses 16 – 18)

II. His Distorted Spirituality (verse 19)

III. His Deadly Shortsightedness (verses 20 – 21)

    a.   There are three rich men in this text.

        i.   The man who requested Jesus's arbitration

        ii. The man in the parable Jesus called "a fool"

        iii. The man who is speaking the parable

            1.   "For ye know the grace of our Lord Jesus Christ, that, though he was rich, yet for your sakes

he became poor that ye through his poverty might be rich" (2 Corinthians 8:9).

2. How rich is our Lord?

– 26 –

The Gift of Gratitude

Luke 17:17-19 [12 – 19] (MSG)

[17] Jesus said, "Were not ten healed? Where are the nine? [18] Can none be found to come back and give glory to God except this outsider?" [19] Then he said to him, "Get up. On your way. Your faith has healed and saved you."

The account of the healing of the ten lepers is unique to the Gospel of Luke. It occurs only once in the Gospels and only here. It has been said that, "First among the things to be thankful for is a thankful spirit ... what a triumph of grace to be made thankful through a renewed heart." This anonymous author noted, "That some people would grumble at the accommodations of heaven if they got there." Our text reminds us that gratitude is not a given but a gift. Sometimes, it manifests itself in the most unlikely of recipients.

I.   The Setting of the Gift of Gratitude (verse 12 – 13)

II.   The Source of the Gift of Gratitude (verse 14)

III. The Stewardship of the Gift of Gratitude (verses 15 - 16)

IV. The Strength of the Gift of Gratitude (verses 17 – 19)

a.   *"And he said unto him, Arise, go thy way: **thy faith hath made thee whole.**"*

"Thank You Lord,
Thank You Lord,
Thank You Lord,
I just want to Thank You Lord!" (Negro Spiritual)

– 27 –

He Came to His Own

John 1:11-12 [1-13] (KJV)

¹¹ He came unto his own, and his own received him not. ¹² But as many as received him, to them gave he power to become the sons of God, *even* to them that believe on his name:

The prologue or introduction to the Gospel of John addresses preliminary matters that are central to the truths communicated in the Gospel. John writes with the aim of encouraging faith in the Son of God.

A few years ago, a pastor shared with me about how he was going through a very difficult time. He said, "I wish God would come and see about me." I thought to myself, "He already has!" His statement was tantamount to the disciples on the stormy sea asking, "Master, carest thou not that we perish?" (Mark 4:38). At the heart of the Christian Gospel is the belief that God has come to see about us.

I. The Revelation of a Great Truth (*"He came"*)

II. The Record of a Great Tragedy (*"His own received him not"*)

III. The Reality of a Great Transaction (*"But as many as received Him"*)

IV. The Rewards of a Great Trustworthiness (*"gave He power to become the sons of God"*)

"There is a tide in the affairs of men,
Which, taken at the flood, leads on to fortune,
Omitted, all the voyage of their life
Is bound in shallows and miseries.
On such a full sea are we now afloat;
And we must take the current when it serves,
Or lose our ventures." (William Shakespeare)

An Inside Job
(An Advent Message)

John 1:10-13 (NIV)

[10] He was in the world, and though the world was made through him, the world did not recognize him. [11] He came to that which was his own, but his own did not receive him. [12] Yet to all who received him, to those who believed in his name, he gave the right to become children of God-- [13] children born not of natural descent, nor of human decision or a husband's will, but born of God.

It is generally assumed that there is no nativity or birth narrative in the Gospel of John. The recounting of the birth of the Christ child is strictly the province of the Gospels of Matthew and Luke – but not John. But the passage before us refutes this position. It presents a Divine trajectory that reaches back into eternity past and then intersects humanity at our deepest and most desperate point of need. God is not some distant, detached deity but, in and through His Son came to this planet to work out our salvation from the inside out.

I. The Greatest Truth (verse 10)

II. The Greatest Tragedy (verse 11)

III. The Greatest Transformation (verses 12 -13)

> "Oh, there are heavenly heights to reach
> In many a fearful place,
> Where the poor timid heir of God
> Lies blindly on his face;
> Lies languishing for grace divine
> That he shall never see
> Till he go forward at Thy sign,
> And trust himself to Thee." (A. L. Waring)

– 29 –

The Satisfaction of Serving

John 2:9-10 [5-10] (NIV)

[9] and the master of the banquet tasted the water that had been turned into wine. He did not realize where it had come from, though the servants who had drawn the water knew. Then he called the bridegroom aside [10] and said, "Everyone brings out the choice wine first and then the cheaper wine after the guests have had too much to drink; but you have saved the best till now."

The Hubble Space Telescope faces outward toward space. It takes pictures of planets, stars and galaxies millions of light-years away. Hubble has witnessed stars being born. Hubble has seen stars die. It has seen galaxies that are trillions of miles away from our own. Hubble also has seen comets crash and collide into the gases above Jupiter. Scientists have learned a great deal about space from the beautiful and breath-taking pictures that the Hubble has taken.

Like the Hubble, the life of the true servant demonstrates and reflects the character of Christ. Like the servants in this text, we become the spiritual telescope that others look through to grasp both the immensity and the immediacy of the love of God who came to this earth not as a Sovereign but as a Servant. Upon careful reading and reflection, the servants in this text are not in the background but the foreground or front stage of the text. Their actions are choreographed in the context of a wedding feast where the wine runs out.

I.   They Served with Encouragement (verse 5)

II.   They Served with Empowerment (verses 7-8)

III. They Served with Enlightenment (verse 9b)

IV.   They Served with Enjoyment (verse 10)

    a. It is not the job, it's the joy!

"I am on the battlefield for my Lord,
I'm on the battlefield for my Lord;

I promised Him that I would serve Him till I die.
I'm on the battlefield for my Lord." (Negro Spiritual)

– 30 –
Spiritual Pediatrics

John 3:3-4 [1-8] (KJV)

³ **Jesus answered and said unto him, Verily, verily, I say unto thee, Except a man be born again, he cannot see the kingdom of God. ⁴ Nicodemus saith unto him, How can a man be born when he is old? can he enter the second time into his mother's womb, and be born?**

Pediatrics is the branch of medicine that deals with the medical care of infants, children, and adolescents (from newborn to age 16-21, depending on the country). The word pediatrics is derived from two Greek words PAIDI which means "child" and IATROS which means "doctor" (The Wikipedia Encyclopedia). One of the primary and predominant metaphors in the Word of God descriptive and prescriptive of God's relationship to His people is that of parent and child.

It is this conceptual category that ascends to center stage during the classic exchange and encounter between Jesus and Nicodemus recorded in the third chapter of the Gospel of John.

    I.   The Disability that Dictates It (verses 1 – 3)

    II.   The Dynamics that Distinguishes It (verses 4 – 7)

   III. The Demonstration that Describes It (verse 8)

        a.   What is the new birth like? What is the essence of spiritual pediatrics? It is like the wind. The wind is often used in the Word of God as a metaphor for the Holy Spirit.

            i.   The wind is universal and not local

           ii.   The wind is strong

          iii.   The wind is satisfying

b. In this text, the answer to our problems is figuratively "blowing in the wind." (Bob Dylan)

- 31 -
The Increase in Decrease

John 3:30 [27-30] (KJV)

³⁰ **He must increase, but I *must* decrease.**

John the Baptist gives us a principle, pattern and paradigm for the ages. It is simply this - **there is increase in decrease!** This is especially timely in an age and era when our culture has become so self-centered, self-occupied, self-absorbed and experiencing in pandemic proportions what I call "increase intoxication." The mantra and motto for our troubling times is "get all you can and can all you get!"

It is reported that Alex Haley, the author of the generational anthology Roots, kept for years a picture in his office showing a turtle sitting atop a fence. When visitors asked him about it, he would say, "The picture is there to remind me of a lesson I learned long ago, if you see a turtle on a fence post, you know he had some help getting there." This text is John's version of the turtle on the fencepost. HE MUST INCREASE BUT I MUST DECREASE.

I.   He Moved from Gain to Grace (verse 27)

II. He Moved from Self to Savior (verse 28)

III. He Moved from Job to Joy (verse 29)

A Major Note in a Minor Key

John 6:8-9 (NIV)

[8] Another of his disciples, Andrew, Simon Peter's brother, spoke up, [9] "Here is a boy with five small barley loaves and two small fish, but how far will they go among so many?"

It is the mid-point of the ministry of Jesus. The Twelve have returned from their mission tour. His popularity blossoming, crowds were teeming around Him and clamoring to hear and see Him. This miracle is narrated in all four of the Gospel narratives. In light of this fact alone, surely none will disagree with me that this miracle is a critical part of the presentation of the life and times of the LORD. If it was a musical score, this passage would undoubtedly be a "major note" in his ministry. But the major note is set in a MINOR KEY.

Each Gospel reports that it was a lad or a child; a minor if you will whose lunch was the basis of the miraculous meal that the Lord would provide to the masses of people who had gathered at this point to hear Him teach. The word translated "boy" in our text or "lad" in the KJV is used to describe a young child. Obviously, a minor is in view here. With this lad as its focal point, could not Jesus be teaching us something about the worth and wealth of our children? This minor was used by God for three reasons.

I. He was Present (*"Here is a boy"*)

II. He was Prudent (*"with five small barley loaves and two small fish"*)

III. He was Productive (*verse 11a* – *"and Jesus took the loaves"*)

Recipe for a Miracle
(An Alternative Exposition (Development) of the Miracle of the Feeding)

John 6:10-13 (NIV)

[10] Jesus said, "Have the people sit down." There was plenty of grass in that place, and the men sat down, about five thousand of them. [11] Jesus then took the loaves, gave thanks, and distributed to those who were seated as much as they wanted. He did the same with the fish. [12] When they had all had enough to eat, he said to his disciples, "Gather the pieces that are left over. Let nothing be wasted." [13] So they gathered them and filled twelve baskets with the pieces of the five barley loaves left over by those who had eaten.

A few years ago, I discovered a recipe for **"brown sugar asparagus."** When I reviewed the ingredients, I had a number of questions most notably, "What's with the chicken broth? I got the butter, the asparagus spears, and the light brown sugar but, chicken broth? I stayed on script and when I shared it with the family; they couldn't get enough of it. So often we miss blessings because we are trying to change or improve upon God's recipe. In the miracle of the feeding of the multitude (five thousand men not counting women and children) recorded in all four Gospels, Jesus provides a recipe for a miracle. There are five ingredients in this miracle entree.

I. Recognize Our Inadequacy (*We Don't Have Enough*)

II. Revise Our Inventory (*We Don't See Enough*)

III. Respect Our Interrelationships (*We Don't Cooperate Enough*)

IV. Release Our Insecurities (*We Don't Believe Enough*)

    a. Give whatever we have, however meager or miserable to the Lord and watch Him work! What are you holding on to that you need to release or relinquish to God?

V. Retain Our Increase (*We Don't Save Enough*)

    a. Some of the best meals and delicacies are those that are warmed up and warmed over. The seasonings have time to saturate the food! This miracle ends with Jesus commanding the disciples to gather up what remains. We are called to do the same. How faithful are we with the *fragments*?

– 34 –
Daybreaks and Nightfalls

John 9:1-4 (KJV)

¹ And as *Jesus* passed by,
he saw a man which was blind from *his* birth.
² And his disciples asked him, saying, Master, who did sin,
this man, or his parents, that he was born blind? ³ Jesus
answered, Neither hath this man sinned, nor his parents: but
that the works of God should be made manifest in him.
⁴ I must work the works of him that sent me, while it is day:
the night cometh, when no man can work.

Our lives are a series of daybreaks and nightfalls. We live between what Linda Ellis describes in her excellent poem, "the dash." We live with the certainty of uncertainty. The disciples attempted to rationalize this man's suffering as caused by some generational curse. Jesus leads them to a higher plateau of understanding.

    I. The Reality of an Unavoidable Problem (*"a man which was blind from his birth"*)

    II. The Reminder of an Undeniable Purpose (*"but that the works of God should be made manifest in him"*)

    III. The Recognition of an Unparalleled Provision (*"I must work the works of him that sent me, while it is day"*)

        a. Jesus can work through and beyond the nightfall of our trials and tribulations. Why and how can this be? Zacharias, the father of John the Baptist, formerly blinded and now blessed pushes through the darkness of his own lack of faith and understanding and gives us the answer in his magnificent prayer! "Through the tender mercy of our God; whereby the dayspring from on high hath visited us" (Luke 1:78).

– 35 –

The Abundant Life
(A New Year's Message)

John 10:9-11 (KJV)

[9] I am the door: by me if any man enter in, he shall be saved, and shall go in and out, and find pasture.
[10] The thief cometh not, but for to steal, and to kill, and to destroy: I am come that they might have life, and that they might have *it* more abundantly.
[11] I am the good shepherd: the good shepherd giveth his life for the sheep.

A sign on the back of a SUV summoned my attention. It read quite simply and succinctly – *"Life is good."* My immediate reaction was silent applause for the positive and optimistic outlook of the vehicle owner who chose those words as a moving and mobile commercial for all eyes to see. However, I quickly was summoned back to reality for I was on my way to a funeral. I thought, "How would the family that I was going to support in the wake of an unexpected loss feel about this affirmation?" Is the death of someone you love during the holidays really good? At that point, the questions began careening into my consciousness. "What of the cancer patient, the recently divorced, the father whose daughter was killed by a hit and run driver, the unemployed, the financially bankrupt, the abused child or spouse, or those suffering under the tyranny of religious oppression or the specter of terrorism?" Is life good for them? What about you or me today?

Would the affirmation "life is good" summarize how you feel now and your outlook for the days that are ahead of you and me in this New Year? Life all by itself is not good but life lived in relationship to Jesus Christ, the Shepherd of our souls is truly good! This life is presented in the Bible as the birthright of every child of God. One of the most compelling descriptions of this life is in our text.

I. It Is the Life Offered <u>with</u> Us (*"I am come"*)

II. It Is the Life Offered <u>to</u> Us (*"that they might have life"*)

III. It Is the Life Offered <u>for</u> Us (*"the good shepherd giveth his life for the sheep"*)

> *"He was born in an obscure village, the son of a peasant woman.*
>
> *He grew up in another village, where he worked in a carpenter's shop until he was thirty. Then for three years he became a wandering preacher.*
>
> *He never wrote a book. He never held an office. He never had a family or owned a house. He didn't go to college. He never visited a big city. He never travelled two hundred miles from the place where he was born. He did none of those things one usually associates with greatness.*
>
> *He had no credentials but himself. He was only thirty-three when the tide of public opinion turned against him. His friends ran away. He was turned over to his enemies and went through a mockery of a trial. He was executed by the state. While he was dying, his executioners gambled for his clothing, the only property he had on earth. When he was dead he was laid in a borrowed grave through the pity of a friend.*
>
> *Twenty centuries have come and gone, and today he is the central figure of the human race and the leader of mankind's progress. All the armies that ever marched, all the navies that ever sailed, all the parliaments that ever*

sat, all the kings that ever reigned, put together, have not affected the life of man on this earth as much as that One Solitary Life." (Author Unknown)

– 36 –

When Jesus Shows Up

John 11:1-4 [17, 43-44] (KJV)

[1] Now a certain *man* was sick, *named* Lazarus, of Bethany, the town of Mary and her sister Martha. [2] (It was *that* Mary which anointed the Lord with ointment, and wiped his feet with her hair, whose brother Lazarus was sick.) [3] Therefore his sisters sent unto him, saying, Lord, behold, he whom thou lovest is sick. [4] When Jesus heard *that*, he said, This sickness is not unto death, but for the glory of God, that the Son of God might be glorified thereby.

The raising of Lazarus from the dead is the seventh and greatest sign performed by our Lord in the Gospel of John. The miracles Jesus performed were his *calling cards*. They accentuated His divinity; that He was co-equal and co-eternal with the Father.

I.   He Shows Up in Our Problems (verses 1 – 2)

II. He Shows Up in Our Prayers (verse 3)

III. He Shows Up in Our Perspectives (verse 4)

IV. He Shows Up in Our Prisons (*context*)

– 37 –

The Tell of the Tears

John 11:35 (KJV)

[35] Jesus wept.

Nothing is so expressive or demonstrative of deep emotion as tears. The late Winston Churchill once spoke of the "persuasive language of a tear." There are tears of joy as well as tears of remorse and sorrow. Tears have been associated not only with great success but great failure as well. What do Jesus's tears tell us?

I.   The Tears Tell Us of the God Who Came

II. The Tears Tell Us of the God Who Cares

III. The Tears Tell Us of the God Who Can

> *"God of our weary years,*
> *God of our silent tears,*
> *Thou who hast brought us thus far on the way*
> *Thou who hast by thy might,*
> *Led us into the light,*
> *Keep us forever in the path we pray."* (James Weldon Johnson)

– 38 –

Sir, We Would See Jesus

John 12:20-21 [20-26] (KJV)

20 And there were certain Greeks among them that came up to worship at the feast: 21 The same came therefore to Philip, which was of Bethsaida of Galilee, and desired him, saying, Sir, we would see Jesus.

American poet and philosopher Henry David Thoreau asked a searching question, "Could a greater miracle happen than for us to look through each other's eyes for an instant?" This text offers a tantalizing possibility for anyone who listens to its heartbeat. On a deeply spiritual level, we can see Jesus. It doesn't matter if we are black or white, rich or poor, white or blue collar, educated or uneducated, liberal or conservative, or saint or sinner, we can see Jesus. Embedded in the movements of this text is not only the possibility but the prescription.

I.   We Can See Him in the Attraction of His Person
     (verses 20 – 22)

II.   We Can See Him in the Activity of His Passion
       (verses 23 – 25)

III.   We Can See Him in the Anticipation of His Preeminence
       (verse 26)

"More about Jesus on His throne,
Riches in glory all His own,
More of His kingdom's sure increase,
More of His coming- Prince of Peace." (Eliza Hewitt)

– 39 –

God's Pay Per View
(An Alternative Development (Exposition) of the Greeks' Inquiry)

John 12:20-22 [20-26] (NIV)

[20] Now there were some Greeks among those who went up to worship at the Feast. [21] They came to Philip, who was from Bethsaida in Galilee, with a request. "Sir," they said, "we would like to see Jesus." [22] Philip went to tell Andrew; Andrew and Philip in turn told Jesus.

Pay-per-view (PPV) is a type of pay television service by which a subscriber of a television service provider can purchase events to view via private telecast. The channel or sponsor shows the event at the same time to everyone ordering it (as opposed to video-on-demand systems, which allow viewers to see recorded broadcasts at any time). Events can be purchased using an on-screen guide, by telephone or through a live customer service representative. Events often include feature films, sporting events and a variety of other entertainment programs.

In the spiritual realm, this text constitutes a kind of pay per view situation. God the Father is the service provider and Jesus is the subscriber. All of humanity has been invited to view the climatic salvation event which culminates with the Son of God hanging helplessly and hopelessly on the Cross and literally screaming out, "My God, My God, why hast thou forsaken me?"(Mark 15:34)

I.   Sacrifice – The Mystery of the Cross (verses 20-24)

II. Surrender – The Message of the Cross (verse 25)

III. Serving – The Ministry of the Cross (verse 26)

> "Dr. Albert Schweitzer (1875 – 1965) shocked his friends and loved ones when he walked away from a distinguished career in theology and music to become a missionary and doctor in the heart of Africa. He refused to listen to the appeals of his friends to stay in Europe. Years later, when he visited America even the most hardened reporters were awed by the sight of the brawny but gentle doctor. One of them asked whether he regretted his sacrifice for the natives of Africa. He responded, 'There was no sacrifice, I am one of the greatly privileged."
> (Robert Payne, <u>The Three Worlds of Albert Schweitzer</u>, 1957)

– 40 –

Good News About an Old Enemy
(Another Alternative Development (Exposition)
of the Greeks' Inquiry)

John 12:24 (KJV)

[24] **Verily, verily, I say unto you, Except a corn of wheat fall into the ground and die, it abideth alone: but if it die, it bringeth forth much fruit.**

Greeks wanted to *see* (translated *see* from the Greek word HORAO; the word from which we get our English word *horizon*) Jesus. This verb communicates the idea of persistent perception.

There is no mere casual interest here, shallow academic speculation or cursory inspection but thoughtful consideration that would lead to thorough transformation.

Jesus responds to their inquiry with the mysterious musings and message of paradox reminding us that those who experience *the crown of Christian victory* must be willing to endure *the cross of Christian suffering*. The death of Jesus Christ on the Cross and His glorious resurrection from the grave completely annihilated the old enemy of our struggle – Death. Jesus used the enemy to affect his demise.

I.   The Principle of Death as a Providential Pattern *("Except a grain of wheat fall into ground and die, it abideth alone ...")*

II. The Prerogative of Death as a Purposeful Prerequisite *("but if it die")*

III. The Potential of Death as a Pleasing Prospect *("it bringeth forth much fruit")*

"Do not stand at my grave and weep.
I am not there, I do not sleep.
I am a thousand winds that blow.
I am the diamond glint on snow.
I am the sunlight on ripened grain.
I am the gentle autumn rain.
When you wake in the morning hush,
I am the swift, uplifting rush
Of quiet birds in circling flight.
I am the soft starlight at night.
Do not stand at my grave and cry.
I am not there, I did not die." (Author Unknown).

What's Love Got to Do with It?

John 13:34-35 (KJV)

[34] A new commandment I give unto you, That ye love one another; as I have loved you, that ye also love one another. [35] By this shall all *men* know that ye are my disciples, if ye have love one to another.

The expositional development of this text should not be viewed as a cinematic expose' on the 1993 movie starring Laurence Fishburne and Angela Bassett about the life of pop singer Tina Turner. Nor is this message a musical critique of the signature single *What's Love God to Do with It* by Tina Turner. But it can be argued that the question raised by the title is relevant and urgent for all Christians and churches. What's love got to do with it?

I.   The Commandment Demands It (*"a new commandment I give unto you"*)

II. The Church Demonstrates It (*By this shall all men know that ye are my disciples"*)

III. The Comforter Develops It (*context in Upper Room Discourse*)

IV. The Cross Declares It (see verse 34b, *"as I have loved you"*)

> *"Jesus loves me this I know,*
> *For the Bible tells me so;*
> *Little ones to Him belong,*
> *They are weak but He is strong."* (William Bradbury)

What Makes Jesus So Special?

John 14:6 [1-7] (NIV)

[6] Jesus answered, "I am the way and the truth and the life.
No one comes to the Father except through me.

The fourth Gospel illuminates the uniqueness of Jesus Christ. Seven times in this Gospel, Jesus uses the "I Am" statement to affirm His eternal essence and unparalleled divinity. This statement is equivalent to what God revealed to Moses in Exodus 3:6, 14. Jesus is the Bread of Life (6:48), Light of the World (8:12), Door to the Sheepfold (10:9), Good Shepherd (10:11), Resurrection and Life (11:25) and True Vine (15:1). In this passage, He is the "Way, the Truth and the Light." His exclusivity is not debatable. While this text is immediately pastoral, it is imminently apologetic in tone and tenor. Jesus has no equals except in the Triune essence of Father, Son and Holy Spirit. Four characteristics in this text make Jesus special.

I.   The Path *("the Way")* that Inspires Our Purpose

II.   The Principle *("the Truth")* that Informs Our Perspective

III.   The Provision *("the Life")* that Invites Our Participation

IV.   The Person *("but by Me")* that Insures Our Pardon

Claiming Our Destiny
(An Alternative Exposition (Development) of John 14:1-7 – An Easter Message)

John 14:3 (NIV)

[3] And if I go and prepare a place for you, I will come back and take you to be with me that you also may be where I am.

This text is a marvelous, moving and monumental reminder to every child of God of our ultimate destiny. It is A PREVIEW OF COMING ATTRACTIONS. The KJV rendering of verse 3 has Jesus saying to the disciples and by extension us,

"And If I go and prepare a place for you, I will come again and receive you unto myself, that where I am, there ye may be also." What a promise! What a possibility! This promise is quite unlike the epitaph on the headstone of a grave in a British cemetery which read,

"Pause my friend, as you walk by
As you are now, so once was I
As I am now so you will be
Prepare my friend, to follow me.
A visitor added,
To follow you is not my intent
Until I know which way you went!" (Author Unknown)

On Easter or Resurrection Sunday, we celebrate because we KNOW WHICH WAY HE WENT. And today is an opportunity to claim or reclaim our destiny as believers.

I.   The Perspective that Calms Our Doubts (verse 1)

II. The Place that Captures Our Dreams (verse 2a)

III. The Promise that Compels Our Determination (verses 2b–3)

IV. The Path that Controls Our Destiny (verses 4-6)

– 44 –

What a Friend We Have in Jesus!

John 15:15 [12-17] (KJV)

[15] Henceforth I call you not servants;
for the servant knoweth not what his lord doeth:
but I have called you friends; for all things that I have heard
of my Father I have made known unto you.

The words friend or friendship have suffered much from our contemporary propensity to use the terms too lightly. Every acquaintance or associate is not a friend. Some people can appreciate your destination but only a small number understand the "journey." True friends and authentic friendship are gifts from God. And then, there is a "friend that sticks closer than a brother"(Proverbs 18:24). I believe that the Wisdom writer had Jesus in mind when he penned those words. Jesus is that kind of Friend!

I.   The Critical Context

II. The Compelling Characteristics

    a. Inviting intimacy

    b. Dynamic disclosure

    c. Extraordinary election

    d. Promising productivity

    e. Commanding communication

III. The Costly Condition

– 45 –

Celebrating the Finish of the Start and the Start of the Finish

John 19:30 (KJV)

[30] When Jesus therefore had received the vinegar, he said, It is finished: and he bowed his head, and gave up the ghost.

In Christian theology, the Cross is the epicenter; the watershed; ground zero; it stands at the most crucial intersection of human history. It defines everything that goes before it and determines everything that follows in its wake.

Every finish has a start and every start has a finish. Finish and start are different sides of the same coin. To consider one without deference to the other is like trying to talk about a one-ended stick.

This text is one of the seven "last words or utterances" of Jesus from the Cross. It is in fact the sixth utterance. Jesus is not the whining, wobbling victim of His captors but the True Viceroy and Victor. These words are not the rant of resignation but the regalia of royalty.

I. The Finish of the Start (*"He said, It is finished"*)

    a. A suffering Servant

    b. A satisfied Sovereign

II. The Start of the Finish (*"He bowed his head, and gave up the ghost"*)

    a. A stunning Salutation

    b. A strategic Surrender

"Were you there when they crucified my Lord? (Were you there?)
Were you there when they crucified my Lord? (Were you there?)
Oh sometimes, it causes me to tremble, tremble, tremble,
Were you there when they crucified my Lord?"

(Negro Spiritual)

– 46 –

From the Innermost to the Uttermost

Acts 1:8 [1-11] (KJV)

[8] **But ye shall receive power, after that the Holy Ghost is come upon you: and ye shall be witnesses unto me both in Jerusalem, and in all Judaea, and in Samaria, and unto the uttermost part of the earth.**

The Gospel of Luke and the Book of Acts is a two-volume work by the same author. It records the evolution of Christianity from the cradle of Judaism into a world religion. What begins in the innermost extends to the uttermost. The Book of Acts ends with the Apostle Paul under house arrest in Rome but the Gospel is "unhindered." This historical anal of early Christianity records the transformation of worship, the spiritual reality that produces integrity to witnessing, and the external response that impacts and influences the world in which we live.

I.   The Proofs that Confirm (verses 1 – 3)

II.   The Promise that Completes (verses 4 – 7)

III. The Power that Compels (verse 8)

IV. The Prospect that Captivates (verses 9 – 11)

      a.   God changes the world through dedicated people and not a detailed plan.

"When He shall come with trumpet sound,
O may I then in Him be found,
Dressed in His righteousness alone,
Faultless to stand before the throne.

On Christ, the solid Rock I sand
All other ground is sinking sand,
All other ground is sinking sand." (Edward Mote)

– 47 –

Convicted by the Convincing

Acts 1:3-5 (NIV)

³ **After his suffering, he showed himself to these men and gave many convincing proofs that he was alive. He appeared to them over a period of forty days and spoke about the kingdom of God. ⁴ On one occasion, while he was eating with them, he gave them this command: "Do not leave Jerusalem, but wait for the gift my Father promised, which you have heard me speak about. ⁵ For John baptized with water, but in a few days you will be baptized with the Holy Spirit."**

The church more often is CONFLICTED rather than CONVICTED. The preeminent symbol of Christianity is not the cross but the EMPTY TOMB. Jesus suffered, died but rose again on the third day. One of the most compelling arguments for the resurrection is the transformation that took place in the disciples. They were CONVICTED BY THE CONVINCING.

I.   His Experience (verse 3a)

II. Their (the Disciples) Experience (verses 3b-5a)

III. Our (My and Your) Experience (verse 5b)

    a. In his book, <u>100 Meditations on Hope</u>, Wayne A. Lamb writes, *"In the midst of a storm, a little bird was clinging to the limb of a tree, seemingly calm and unafraid. As the wind tore at the limb of the tree, the bird continued to look the storm in the face, as if to say, SHAKE ME OFF; I STILL HAVE MY WINGS."*

    b. My and your experience of the resurrection through the revelatory and the mediatorial ministry of the Holy Spirit should compel us to tell every problem; every heartache; every disease; every difficulty; every trial; disappointment – SHAKE ME OFF BUT I STILL HAVE MY WINGS! I AM CONVICTED BY THE CONVINCING!

– **48** –

A Church on Fire

Acts 2:3-4 [1-47] (KJV)

[3] **And there appeared unto them cloven tongues like as of fire, and it sat upon each of them.** [4] **And they were all filled with the Holy Ghost, and began to speak with other tongues, as the Spirit gave them utterance.**

God literally poured spiritual charcoal fluid on the church on the Day of Pentecost. What happened fulfilled the promise that Jesus had made to the church prior to His ascension. The gift of the Holy Spirit appeared as cloven tongues of fire and enabled the church's compelling and unhindered witness of the Gospel.

I. A Praying Church (verse 1)

II. A Powerful Church (verses 2 – 4)

III. A Preaching Church (verses 5 – 40)

    a. Compelling centrality

    b. Committed couriers

    c. Commanding clarity

    d. Christological content

    e. Convicting consequences

IV. A Purposeful Church (verses 41 -46)

V. A Praising Church (verse 47a)

VI. A Progressive Church (verse 47b)

    a. There is a brand of charcoal that is self-igniting; no need for lighter fluid. This should be the spiritual condition of every child of God. We should be *Match Light* Christians!

– 49 –

The Day the Church Caught Fire
(An Alternative Exposition (Development of Acts 2:1-13)

Acts 2:3-4 [1-13] (KJV)

[3] And there appeared unto them cloven tongues like as of fire, and it sat upon each of them. [4] And they were all filled with the Holy Ghost, and began to speak with other tongues, as the Spirit gave them utterance.

The Book of Acts is a *baby picture* of the church; it records the dynamics surrounding the infancy of the church. Their courageous and consistent example of faith and fortitude should encourage the contemporary church so muddled in malaise and mediocrity to catch on fire.

I. A Prayerful Partnership

II. A Powerful Provision

III. A Pleasing Pattern

IV. A Provocative Proclamation

– 50 –
The Priorities of a Praying Church
Acts 2:42 (KJV)

⁴² And they continued stedfastly in the apostles' doctrine and fellowship, and in breaking of bread, and in prayers.

The contemporary church is suffering from amnesia and anorexia in the area of prayer. It reminds me of the story of two men who were chiding each other about knowing the Model Prayer. One man said to the other, "I'll bet you $10 that you can't recite it!" The other man responded to the challenge and said, "Now I lay me down to sleep, I pray the Lord my soul to keep, if I die before I wake, I pray the Lord my soul to take." The other man took $10 from his pocket and paid him!

This text reminds us of the church's essential and non-negotiable priorities. Ignore them, and we can become like the small church in the city that closed and placed on its doors a sign that said, *"Gone out of business because we didn't know what our business was."*

I. Commendable Cooperation in a Serving Community (verses 41-42a)

II. Consistent Commitment to a Supernatural Curriculum (verse 42b)

III. Compelling Confirmation of the Savior's Confidence (verses 43-47)

    a. Awe

    b. Acceptance

    c. Adoration

    d. Addition

– 51 –

What Happens When Our Church Becomes the Lord's Church?

Acts 2:42-47 [1-47] (NIV)

[42] They devoted themselves to the apostles' teaching and to the fellowship, to the breaking of bread and to prayer. [43] Everyone was filled with awe, and many wonders and miraculous signs were done by the apostles. [44] All the believers were together and had everything in common. [45] Selling their possessions and goods, they gave to anyone as he had need. [46] Every day they continued to meet together in the temple courts. They broke bread in their homes and ate together with glad and sincere hearts, [47] praising God and enjoying the favor of all the people. And the Lord added to their number daily those who were being saved.

Acts 2 is a "back to basics" account of the development and growth of the early church. In context, each paragraph of the chapter moves like a strong, torrential current down the river that empties into an ocean of possibility for church leaders and members who hear and heed its principles and priorities.

I.   The Power that Propels the Church

II. The Preaching that Permeates the Church

III. The Priorities that Perfect the Church

IV. The PERSON that Prospers the Church

– 52 –

Settling on the Premises or Standing on the Promises

Acts 3:8 [1-10] (NIV)

[8] He jumped to his feet and began to walk. Then he went with them into the temple courts, walking and jumping, and praising God.

This passage is pertinent to those who occupy residence, domicile and hiatus in holy places. There is the story of the father who visited his son at a prestigious private college in the East. The father is walking across campus and spots his son's math professor. He says to him, "My son took math from you." The professor responds. "He was exposed to it; but he didn't take it!" Too many are exposed to Christianity but "don't take it!" and therefore "don't make it!" This text moves down two corridors - the problems at the gate and the possibilities beyond the gate.

I. His Fatal Flaw (verses 1 – 2a)

   a. He was crippled from his birth

II. His Fruitless Friendships (verse 2b)

   a. Some friendships are socially stimulating but spiritually stagnating; why didn't his friends take him beyond the gate?

   b. Spiritual growth sometimes requires the "rapturous rupture of relationships."

III. His Fractured Fellowship (verse 2c)

IV. His Frivolous Fulfillment (verses 2d)

   a. This man became satisfied with the "noise in the cup."

V. His Fortifying Faith (verses 3 – 10)

   a. But when he stood up by faith on the promises of God, he experienced …

      i. The privileges of a praying church

      ii. The work and worth of a witnessing church

      iii. The blessing of a believing church

What's in a Name?
(An Advent Message)

Acts 4:12 (NIV)

[12] **Salvation is found in no one else, for there is no other name under heaven given to men by which we must be saved."**

In the ancient world, the name of someone was inextricably intertwined with his or her essence. To know their name was to be able to exert power over or engage the power of someone or something. In the primeval innocence of the Garden, God gave authority to Adam to name the creatures brought before him. That privilege signaled Adam's authority and dominion over the created order. In his 1968 book, The Pedagogy of the Oppressed, the Latin American theologian Paulo Friere argues that what makes us authentically human is the God-given right to name our creation or environment.

The Christmas season affords the church the opportunity to reflect upon our relationship to the One whose "name is above every name." What's in a name?

I. An Exclusive Claim (*"neither is their salvation in any other"*)

II. An Exceptional Contribution (*"for there is none other name given among men"*)

III. An Essential Condition (*"whereby we must be saved"*)

Guilty by Association

Acts 4:13-14 (KJV)

[13] Now when they saw the boldness of Peter and John, and perceived that they were unlearned and ignorant men, they marvelled; and they took knowledge of them, that they had been with Jesus. [14] And beholding the man which was healed standing with them, they could say nothing against it.

A few months ago, I was watching an episode of *First 48* on the A&E channel. The setting was Miami-Dade County, Florida. A murder investigation was underway. In order to break the case in the first forty-eight hours, the detectives interviewed witnesses, followed leads and interrogated suspects. A break in the case occurred; the investigation focused in on a sixteen-year old who, while not the shooter was complicit in the crime. He was guilty by association.

Likewise, there is an important issue breached in this passage; certainly one that is relevant to the contemporary church and to any church striving for excellence in Christian ministry. The church is increasingly vulnerable to those who would challenge and criticize her ministry and mission. In this text, the religious leaders in their attempt to stifle and stop the church from witnessing about Jesus could only conclude when they examined Peter and John in particular that THEY HAD BEEN WITH JESUS. They were guilty by association on five counts.

I. They were Compelled by their Connection (verse 13)

II. They were Energized by their Exposure (verse 13)

III. They were Motivated by their Mission (verse 14)

IV. They were Strengthened by their Struggles (*context*)

Designer Christiantiy

Acts 4:13-14 (NIV)

¹³ When they saw the courage of Peter and John and realized that they were unschooled, ordinary men, they were astonished and they took note that these men had been with Jesus. ¹⁴ But since they could see the man who had been healed standing there with them, there was nothing they could say.

Amidst the imposters and pretenders that inhabit the landscape of the contemporary church, it is way past time to do an inspection and check the designer label that distinguishes Christianity from all other religions. When the Jewish leaders checked the spiritual apparel of the apostles, they could only conclude that *they had been with Jesus.* Designer Christianity is biblically based and Christ-centered. What are the characteristics of designer Christianity?

I.   A Courageous Commitment (verse 13a)

II. A Clear Connection (verse 13b)

III. A Compelling Confirmation (verse 14)

    a. "For the man who was miraculously healed was over forty years old" (verse 22).

What's Up with the Prayer Meeting?

Acts 4:31 (KJV)

³¹ And when they had prayed, the place was shaken where they were assembled together; and they were all filled with the Holy Ghost, and they spake the word of God with boldness.

Prayer is a central theme in both Luke and Acts. In the Gospel of Luke, Jesus enters the city of Jerusalem triumphantly (Luke 19:36ff). He cleanses the Temple and then announces, "My house is the house of prayer but you have made it a den of thieves" (Luke 19:46). In Acts, the church begins in a prayer meeting not a church board meeting or a business meeting.

I. A Praying Church Has a Hook-Up (*"And when they had prayed"*)

II. A Praying Church Has a Shake-Up (*"and the place was shaken where they assembled together"*)

III. A Praying Church Has a Fill-Up (*"and they were all filled with the Holy Ghost"*)

IV. A Praying Church Has a Speak-Up (*"and the spake the word of God with boldness"*)

> *"Sweet hour of prayer, sweet hour of prayer,*
> *May I thy consolation share,*
> *Till from Mount Pisgah's lofty heights*
> *I view my home and take my flight*
> *And shout, while passing through the air,*
> *'Farewell, farewell, sweet hour of prayer."* (William W. Walford)

– 57 –

The Arithmetic of a Growing Church

Acts 6:7 [1-7] (KJV)

⁷ And the word of God increased; and the number of the disciples multiplied in Jerusalem greatly; and a great company of the priests were obedient to the faith.

God expects His church to grow; a church that is not growing is stagnant or dying. Church growth in the Book of Acts is both compelling and *calculated*. This passage bears witness of this truth. It addresses the area of spiritual arithmetic. The dictionary defines "arithmetic" as the science of computing numbers and embraces addition, subtraction, division and multiplication. We must find the appropriate balance between the idolatry of the numeric and the ignorance of the numeric.

I. Multiplication Leads to Division *("in those days the number of the disciples was multiplied")*

II. Division Leads to Subtraction *("it is not reason that we should leave the Word of God, and serve tables")*

III. Subtraction Leads to Addition *("Wherefore, brethren, look ye out among you seven men")*

IV. Addition Leads to Multiplication *("And the Word of God increased; and the number of disciples multiplied")*

– 58 –

Straight Talk on Straight Street

Acts 9:11-12 [10-22] (NIV)

[11] The Lord told him, "Go to the house of Judas on Straight Street and ask for a man from Tarsus named Saul, for he is praying. [12] In a vision he has seen a man named Ananias come and place his hands on him to restore his sight."

The Dictionary (McGraw-Hill Dictionary of American Idioms and Phrasal Verbs © 2002) defines *straight talk* as "direct and honest talk." It is what our young people mean today when they say, "keeping it real." My generation would call a person who engaged in honest and unembellished conversation a "straight-shooter."

Some straight talk took place during the infancy of the church on a street called "Straight" in the city of Damascus. That conversation not only left its indelible footprint on two men but it transformed the church and changed the world!

I. The Savior Behind the Scene (verses 10-12)

II. The Servant At the Scene (verses 13-17)

III. The Spirit Inside the Scene (verse 18)

The Power of a Praying Church

Acts 12:5 [1-11] (KJV)

5 Peter therefore was kept in prison: but prayer was made without ceasing of the church unto God for him.

Prayer is pivotal in the Book of Acts. The book is permeated with a pattern of prayer. The church was birthed in a prayer meeting (Acts 2); Peter and John enter the Temple at the hour of prayer (Acts 3); the disciples pray for more boldness after being released from prison (Acts 4); in some backstreet of the city of Damascus, Paul prayed (Acts 9); Peter prays on a rooftop (Acts 10); the Church of Antioch prays and set apart Paul and Barnabas as missionaries (Acts 13); Paul and Silas prayed and the jailhouse rocked (Acts 16); Paul prays with and for the Ephesian elders in a teary farewell (Acts 20); and during a storm at sea with Paul as a prisoner on board, sailors dropped four anchors and prayed (Acts 27). In this text, we find the church praying as persecution against her key leaders intensifies.

I.   The Distress that Motivated Their Prayers (verses 1-5a)

II. The Determination that Multiplied Their Prayers (verse 5b)

III. The Deliverance that Magnified Their Prayers (verses 6-11)

A Prime Time Witness in a Subprime World

Romans 1:16 [13-17] (KJV)

16 For I am not ashamed of the gospel of Christ: for it is the power of God unto salvation to every one that believeth; to the Jew first, and also to the Greek.

The Apostle Paul is a "prime time" witness in the New Testament. He towers like some Mt. Everest in the New

Testament; authored thirteen of the twenty-seven books of the New Testament; is a key player in the history and development of the early church as recorded in Acts; his writings reflect genius and substance and ran the gamut from systematic theology (Romans); philosophy (Colossians) to personal instruction and encouragement (Philemon; 2 Timothy).

I was reading an article recently about Paul. It was titled, *"Paul, Insane, Obsessive or Genius."* The article was based on the claims by his critics recorded in Acts and 2 Corinthians that he was mad or out of his mind. Paul responded in 2 Corinthians 5:13 by saying, "For whether we be beside ourselves (insane) or whether we be sober (sound mind), it is for your cause." Paul was an apostle and preacher of the Gospel. I can't help but believe when I am reading his writings in the New Testament that he was under a GO-SPELL. He was driven! And God and the Gospel were doing the driving. He was prime time!

I.   His Passionate Concern (verses 13 - 15)

II. His Powerful Capability (verse 16)

III. His Pleasing Confidence (verse 17)

– 61 –

Winning the War Within

Romans 7:18-21 [7:14-8:1] (KJV)

[18] For I know that in me (that is, in my flesh,) dwelleth no good thing: for to will is present with me; but *how* to perform that which is good I find not. [19] For the good that I would I do not: but the evil which I would not, that I do.
[20] Now if I do that I would not, it is no more I that do it, but sin that dwelleth in me. [21] I find then a law, that, when I would do good, evil is present with me.

There is war raging! Not in Iraq or Afghanistan but much closer to home. Casualties and costs continue to rise. Multitudes have been wounded on the battlefield; lives decimated and families devastated by the losses. Roadside bombs and hidden blasts have maimed and mangled many. There is no sign of a cease fire or the cessation of conflict in the near future. Every Christian is involved in this conflict. It is not geographical or a violent contest and confrontation between nations; it is spiritual; it is not war without but a WAR WITHIN.

The Apostle Paul is a seasoned veteran of this struggle; he is not a pacifist but a realist and perhaps even by some accounts a warmonger. His chronicles of the war in the passage before us and many more are up close and intimately personal. He is not a bystander or a spectator but one who sees and senses the intensity of the conflict.

I.   The War Within Cannot Be Won With Human Reason

II.   The War Within Cannot Be Won With Human Resolve

III. The War Within Cannot Be Won With Human Resources

IV.   The War Within Can Only Be Won With A Heavenly Redeemer

– 62 –

Fast Forwarding Through Life's Reversals

Romans 8:18 (KJV)

[18] **For I reckon that the sufferings of this present time *are* not worthy *to be compared* with the glory which shall be revealed in us.**

My cable service includes a DVR or record function. I have the ability to record programs and watch them later; or even to set up a series recording from week to week. The advantage of course is that I can watch my favorite program commercial free; I can fast forward through the seemingly endless march of commercials.

I thought about how great it would be in life if we could do this. When we experience a reversal, a setback or find ourselves in a difficult place, just to have the ability to grab a remote and fast forward through the pain, the sorrow, the tears, the disappointment or difficulty. So often we find ourselves in life at worst "stopped" and at best "paused" as we experience and endure the inevitable reversals - the trials and tribulations that will surely come. No one here gets a "commercial free" pass or exemption. Sin, sorrow, sickness, suffering and death will advertise on your life channel no matter who you are, what you know, where you live or how much money you have. But there are some ways every child of God can fast forward through these difficult seasons.

I.   Through Application of the Word of God (*"the sufferings of the present time"*)

   a.   The Word of God *establishes our viewpoint.*

   b.   According to the Word of God, suffering has an expiration date!

II.   Through Submission to the Plan of God (*"are not worthy to be compared to the glory"*)

   a.   Submitting to God's plans and purposes for us *encourages our vigilance.*

   b.   See Jeremiah 29:11

III.   Through Revelation of the Promises of God (*"which shall be revealed in us"*)

   a.   Standing on God's promises *enables our vision.*

"Ah! Why by passing clouds oppressed.
Should vexing thoughts distract thy breast?
Turn thou to Him in every pain,
Whom never suppliant sought in vain;
Thy strength in joy's ecstatic day,
Thy hope, when joy has passed away." (H. F. Lyte)

When God Puts Our Circumstances to Work

Romans 8:28 [26-28] (KJV)

[28] And we know that all things work together for good
to them that love God, to them who are the called
according to *his* purpose.

The U. S. economy continues to experience a slow recovery from the catastrophic downturn of 2008. Unemployment is lagging and there are many who believe that this factor is slowing down or threatening a full economic recovery.

Our text makes an astounding claim! When it comes to our circumstances, the unemployment rate is 0%. God is putting our circumstances (whatever they are) to work for our good. I asked the text the question, what happens when God puts our circumstances to work? The text and its context yield four responses.

I.   The Unlimited Character (*"And we know all things"*)

II. The Unprecedented Cooperation (*"work together for good"*)

III. The Uncompromising Conditions (*"to them that love God and are the called according to His purpose"*)

IV. The Unshakeable Conclusion (*"What shall we say to these things? If God be for us, who can be against us?"*)

    a.   Gospel singer and icon, Shirley Caesar says it well,

"Though the pressures of life seem to weigh you down,
And you don't know which way to turn;
God is concerned and He's working it out for you ...

No peace in the home, and no peace on the job,
The bills are due, and your health is failing too;
God is concerned and He's working it out for you."

– 64 –
The Fight is Fixed

Romans 8:31 [28 - 39] (KJV)
[31] **What shall we then say to these things?**
If God *be* **for us, who** *can be* **against us?**

Many expositors believe that the first verse in this passage launches the sensational summary and compelling conclusion of the profound and prolific first eight chapters of the Book of Romans. Paul's arguments have come down to this single, solitary question, IF GOD BE FOR US, WHO CAN BE AGAINST US? In the original language, the phrase translated "If God" is a condition of the first class and means "since" or "because." Because God is on our side, victory is mine and yours. We can say in a commendable and complimentary way, that THE FIGHT IS FIXED.

I.   The Precedents that Signal It (verses 28 – 30)

II.   The Price that Secures It (verses 31 – 34)

III.   The Promises that Settle It (verses 35 – 39)

– 65 –
Giving God Our Best

Romans 12:1-2 (KJV)
[1] **I beseech you therefore, brethren, by the mercies of God,**
that ye present your bodies a living sacrifice, holy,
acceptable unto God, *which is* **your reasonable service.**
[2] **And be not conformed to this world: but be ye transformed**
by the renewing of your mind, that ye may prove what *is* **that**
good, and acceptable, and perfect, will of God.

This chapter is the beginning of the final division in the Book of Romans. For eleven chapters, Paul has engaged his audience with didactic doctrinal declarations and powerful propositional pronouncements, but he is not satisfied with this. The jury is still out as he seeks to move his readers from doctrine to duty. This is the fourth time in the epistle that the Apostle Paul emphasizes doctrinal conclusions by using the word "therefore." The first two verses of this chapter are a clarion call to all who love the Lord that He desires nothing less than our very best.

I.   The Motivation that Demands It (verse 1a)

II.   The Measure that Defines It (verse 1b)

III. The Maturity that Distinguishes It (verse 2a)

IV.   The Model that Demonstrates It (verse 2b and context)

– 66 –

Living with Limited Vision

1 Corinthians 13:12 (KJV)

12 For now we see through a glass, darkly; but then face to face: now I know in part; but then shall I know even as also I am known.

This is the Apostle Paul's great love chapter. It aims to address the dissension, disunity and division in the Corinthian church. As he brings the chapter to a magnificent end he summarily addresses the maturity that love encourages (verse 11); the mystery that love evokes (verse 12) and the magnitude (superiority) that love enjoys among the three primary Christian virtues (verse 13).

Paul's words here remind me of a drive I took recently. As I entered a certain section of the highway, I saw a sign that said, *"Fog warning – reduce speed – low visibility next 5 miles."* How endemic of life that sign is! While, "now we see through a glass darkly," the good news is that when the sun (Son) rises, the fog does lift.

I.   The Pattern of our Perception (*"we see through a glass darkly"*)

II.   The Progression of our Perception (*"but then face to face"*)

III.   The Perfection of our Perception (*"now I know in part; but then shall I know even as also I am known"*)

"*Over my head, I see glory in the air,*
Over my head, I see glory in the air,
Over my head, I see glory in the air,
There must be a God somewhere." (Negro Spiritual)

– 67 –

Blame It on Grace

1 Corinthians 15:10 (NIV)

[10] **But by the grace of God I am what I am, and his grace to me was not without effect. No, I worked harder than all of them-- yet not I, but the grace of God that was with me.**

I am a lover of the classic western movie. One of my all-time favorites is <u>Broken Lance</u> which first hit the theaters in 1954. The movie boasts an all-star cast including Spencer Tracy, Robert Wagner, Jean Peters, Richard Widmark, and E. G. Marshall. Cattle baron Matt Devereaux played by Spencer Tracy and his men raid and destroy a copper mine that is polluting his water and poisoning his cattle. When the case goes to trial, the proud rancher faces jail time and risks losing all unless he divides his property among his four sons which he refuses to do. His favorite son Joe played by Robert Wagner takes the fall or the blame for the raid and gets three years in prison. While Joe is in prison, Matt Devereaux dies from a stroke partly caused by the treachery of Joe's three rebellious brothers. When Joe gets out he plans revenge.

In this verse, the Apostle Paul makes an astounding claim about his life and his ministry. The essence of what he shares is, "when you look at my life, when you look at my ministry, when you look at my peace, joy and contentment – BLAME IT ON GRACE. Here are the things that Paul insists that we blame on grace.

I.   The Soul of His Person

II. The Source of His Passion

III. The Secret of His Production

– 68 –

The Victory Mindset

1 Corinthians 15:54-57 (NIV)

⁵⁴ **When the perishable has been clothed with the imperishable, and the mortal with immortality, then the saying that is written will come true: "Death has been swallowed up in victory." ⁵⁵ "Where, O death, is your victory? Where, O death, is your sting?" ⁵⁶ The sting of death is sin, and the power of sin is the law. ⁵⁷ But thanks be to God! He gives us the victory through our Lord Jesus Christ. ⁵⁸Therefore, my dear brothers, stand firm. Let nothing move you. Always give yourselves fully to the work of the Lord, because you know that your labor in the Lord is not in vain.**

Some of my generation will remember that long before there was ever ESPN or Fox Sports Network, there was a very popular show on television that began with the symphonic shrill of trumpet blasts, with compelling and colorful documentary and the words of the late and legendary broadcaster Jim McKay,

> **"Spanning the globe to bring you the constant variety of sports, the thrill of victory, the agony of defeat; the human drama of athletic competition ... This is ABC's Wide World of Sports!**

This text documents the thrill of victory only; there is no agony of defeat. Three of the six occurrences of the word "victory" in the New Testament are concentrated in this passage. It is a passage that marks the conclusion of the most expansive treatment of the doctrine of resurrection in the Bible. This text and its context encourage every child of God to adopt "the victory mindset." There are three movements in these verses regarding "the victory mindset."

I.   The Promise of the Victory (verse 54)

II. The Pattern of the Victory (verses 55-56)

III. The Provider of the Victory (verse 57)

IV. *Bonus Point!*

     a.   The Proceeds of the Victory (verse 58)

"O victory in Jesus, my Savior forever!
He sought me and bought me
With His redeeming blood;
He loves me ere I knew Him,
And all my love is due Him
He plunged me to victory,
Beneath the cleansing flood." (Eugene M. Bartlett)

– 69 –

Living with a Resurrection Mentality (An Easter Message)

1 Corinthians 15:51-52 [51-58] (NIV)

[51] Listen, I tell you a mystery: We will not all sleep, but we will all be changed-- [52] in a flash, in the twinkling of an eye, at the last trumpet. For the trumpet will sound, the dead will be raised imperishable, and we will be changed.

Alexander Pope wrote, "Hope springs eternal in the human breast; man never is but always to be blest ... *but where does man turn when hope dries up."* Surprisingly, the atheist, Frederick Nietzhe once said, *"He who has a why to live can bear almost any how."*

The truth of the resurrection OUGHT TO impact our daily living. Every child of God should live with a resurrection mentality.

I.   Live with the Awareness of a Compelling Reality (verses 51-57)

II.   Live with the Activity of a Critical Responsibility (verse 58a)

III. Live with the Anticipation of a Comforting Reassurance (verse 58b)

– 70 –

God's Overdraft Protection

2 Corinthians 3:4-6 (KJV)

⁴ And such trust have we through Christ to God-ward: ⁵ Not that we are sufficient of ourselves to think any thing as of ourselves; but our sufficiency *is* of God; ⁶ Who also hath made us able ministers of the new testament; not of the letter, but of the spirit: for the letter killeth, but the spirit giveth life.

The Apostle Paul defends his apostolic and ministerial calling and credentials in his second letter to the church at Corinth. There were some in the congregation who had the audacity to question both. While engaging in this apologetic or defense of his ministry, he affirms something that is true not only of every minister but of every child of God. **Our spiritual, intellectual, relational, emotional and material resources are insufficient to handle the demands that we face in life.** Sooner or later, life will write a bill that is too large to pay and, if we try to write a check to cover it, the check will surely bounce. In these situations, God provides overdraft protection.

I.   We Know More than We See (verse 4)

II.   We Need More than We Have (verse 5)

III. We Receive More than We Earn (verse 6)

The Confidence to Continue

2 Corinthians 3:17-4:1 (KJV)

¹⁷ Now the Lord is that Spirit:
and where the Spirit of the Lord *is*, there *is* liberty.
¹⁸ But we all, with open face beholding as in a glass the glory
of the Lord, are changed into the same image from glory to
glory, *even* as by the Spirit of the Lord. ¹ Therefore seeing we
have this ministry, as we have received mercy, we faint not;

Continuing can always be a challenge. Quitting is always a temptation. Life in all of its multifaceted expressions weighs heavily on us at times and the whisper becomes a shout and the shout becomes a scream and if we are not careful, we will lay down our arms, surrender and walk away. It happens in marriage. We feel that way sometimes as parents. The job and the career offer unique challenges and ministry is not exempt. The Apostle Paul cultivated this capacity. We can learn from his example.

I.   The Person that Frees Us (verse 17)

II.   The Presence that Fashions Us (verse 18)

III. The Provision that Fortifies Us (2 Corinthians 4:1)

The Common Problem of an Uncommon Provision

2 Corinthians 4:7 (KJV)

⁷ But we have this treasure in earthen vessels, that the
excellency of the power may be of God, and not of us.

Who would argue that to be couriers, communicators and containers of the Gospel is an uncommon privilege? The church and every believer have been accorded an inestimable trust. The Apostle Paul reminded Timothy of this hallowed bequest at the very end of his first letter with rapt exhortation, "O Timothy, keep that which is committed to thy trust ..." (1 Timothy 4:20a).

It is very likely that this is the sentiment and sense that gripped the conscience and heart of the hymn writer who said, *"A charge to keep I have, a God to glorify, who gave His son my soul to save, and fit it for the sky"* (Charles Wesley). This passage is a searching reminder that it is not only the content of the Gospel or our calling that unites us but our human condition and context as well. In other words, we are united by the expression of a common faith, the evidence of a common favor, but also the experience of a common fragility or finiteness.

I.   A Discernible Pattern and Participation (*"But we have"*)

II.   A Distinctive Possession and Paradox (*"this treasure in earthen vessels"*)

III. A Dynamic Power and Provision (*"that the excellency of the power may be of God and not of us"*)

– 73 –
Living in Time for Eternity

2 Corinthians 5:1 [4:16-5:1] (KJV)

¹ For we know that if our earthly house of *this* tabernacle were dissolved, we have a building of God, an house not made with hands, eternal in the heavens.

The Book of 2 Corinthians is a systematic defense; an apologetic of the Apostle Paul's ministry. Almost from the beginning of his ministry, skeptics and critics hounded him at every turn. He defended time and time again his apostolic calling and ministry credentials. Chapter 4 begins in a defensive posture but, around verse 16, there is a shift in the textual atmosphere. Paul's vision and view is catapulted beyond the immediate concerns of his ministry into the distant yet distinct horizons of his (and our) ultimate destiny in Christ Jesus. Paul is not looking into a *cracked crystal ball* but revisiting a theme that he breached compellingly and comprehensively in the first epistle to this worrisome congregation that, "If in this life only we have hope in Christ, we are of all men most miserable" (1 Corinthians 15:19). Indeed, the best is yet to come when you and I live in time <u>for</u> eternity!

I. Model the Mystery (2 Corinthians 4:16)
II. Measure the Misery (2 Corinthians 4:17)
III. Master the Material (2 Corinthians 4:18)
IV. Maintain the Motivation (2 Corinthians 5:1)

   a. In December 1941, a nineteen–year old American pilot serving with the Royal Canadian Air Force in England was killed when his Spitfire jet collided with another airplane inside a cloud. Discovered among his personal effects was this poem written on the back of a letter he had not mailed while attending flight school in Farnborough, England.

"Oh! I have slipped the surly bonds of earth,
And danced the skies on laughter-silvered wings;
Sunward I've climbed, and joined the tumbling mirth
Of sun-split clouds, --and done a hundred things
You have not dreamed of --Wheeled and soared and swung
High in the sunlit silence. Hov'ring there
I've chased the shouting wind along, and flung
My eager craft through footless halls of air...
Up, up the long, delirious, burning blue
I've topped the wind-swept heights with easy grace
Where never lark or even eagle flew --
And, while with silent lifting mind I've trod
The high untrespassed sanctity of space,
Put out my hand, and touched the face of God." (John Gillespie Magee, Jr.)

Abounding Through Adversity

2 Corinthians 12:8-9 [7-10] (NIV)

⁸ Three times I pleaded with the Lord to take it away from me.
⁹ But he said to me, "My grace is sufficient for you,
for my power is made perfect in weakness."
Therefore I will boast all the more gladly about my
weaknesses, so that Christ's power may rest on me.

In this text, the "thorn" is generic; a kind of "spiritual fill in the blank." All we need to know is that it "hurts!" We all have something in our life that hurts! That is the source of difficulty. It could be emotional, physical, psychological, financial, relational or spiritual. Thorns are symbolic of our "fallen-ness." Remember, after Adam's transgression in the garden, the ground was cursed. God said, "thorns and thistles shall it [the earth] bring forth" (Genesis 3:18).

But God's permissive will allowed this thorn; God's plan was to use it to help the Apostle Paul. Satan desired to use it to hurt and hinder Paul. The apostle's life was divinely orchestrated; the thorn was given to him. Twice we are told why. He had been the object of extraordinary revelation. The thorn was given to keep him humble. GOD KNOWS WHAT IS BEST FOR US. God promises in Isaiah 49:11 to "turn the mountains into roads." Therefore, we can abound in adversity.

I.   Adversity Exposes the Purposes of God

II. Adversity Energizes the Promises of God

III. Adversity Engages the Power of God

Dealing with God's Denials
(An Alternative Treatment of a Thorny Passage)

2 Corinthians 12:7-9 [1 – 10] (MSG)

[7] Because of the extravagance of those revelations, and so I wouldn't get a big head, I was given the gift of a handicap to keep me in constant touch with my limitations. Satan's angel did his best to get me down; what he in fact did was push me to my knees. No danger then of walking around high and mighty! [8] At first I didn't think of it as a gift, and begged God to remove it. Three times I did that, [9] and then he told me, My grace is enough; it's all you need. My strength comes into its own in your weakness. Once I heard that, I was glad to let it happen. I quit focusing on the handicap and began appreciating the gift. It was a case of Christ's strength moving in on my weakness.

I.   Acknowledge God's Purposes (verse 7)

II. Access God's Power (verses 8 – 9)

III. Appropriate God's Provision (verse 10)

> *"Trials dark on every hand,*
> *And we cannot understand,*
> *All the ways that God will lead us*
> *To that blessed Promised Land,*
> *But He guides us with His eye*
> *And we'll follow till we die.*
> *For we'll understand it better by and by."* (C. A. Tindley)

The Worth in Weakness
(Another Alternative Exposition of a Thorny Passage)

2 Corinthians 12:8-9 [7-10] (NIV)

[8] Three times I pleaded with the Lord to take it away from me.
[9] But he said to me, "My grace is sufficient for you,
for my power is made perfect in weakness."
Therefore I will boast all the more gladly about my
weaknesses, so that Christ's power may rest on me.

Believers witness on a daily basis the grace and power of God at work in our lives transforming our weaknesses into strengths. This is the spiritual legacy that the Apostle Paul leaves us in this text. He is saying for all to hear, "Don't look at me but look at grace." God uses us not because of ourselves but in spite of ourselves.

The saints of old lived with humbling reminders that their greatness and significance were only expressions of God's grace. They found worth in their weakness.

I.   The Reality of Our Weakness (verse 7a; compare 2 Corinthians 4:7)

II.   The Reason for Our Weakness (verse 7b)

III. The Response to Our Weakness (verses 8 – 10)

Winning the War Against Weariness

Galatians 6:9 (KJV)

[9] And let us not be weary in well doing:
for in due season we shall reap, if we faint not.

There was significant news coverage of the 60th Anniversary of D-Day- the massive allied invasion of France that strategically brought World War II to an end. Many soldiers after intense and sustained fighting experienced "combat fatigue."

The audience that the Apostle Paul addresses in this epistle was experiencing a similar phenomenon. He addresses the same words to the church at Thessalonica (see 2 Thessalonians 4:13).

I.   The Persistent Problem ("*And let us not be weary in well doing*")

II. The Pleasing Promise ("*for in due season we shall reap*")

III. The Pressing Prerequisite ("*if we faint not*")

> "*Let us cheer the weary traveler,*
> *Let us cheer the wary traveler,*
> *Along the heavenly way.*" (Negro Spiritual)

– 78 –

The Grammar of Grace

Ephesians 2:8-9 [1-10] (KJV)

[8] **For by grace are ye saved through faith; and that not of yourselves:** *it is* **the gift of God:** [9] **Not of works, lest any man should boast.**

The dictionary defines grammar as the branch of linguistics dealing with the form and structure of words (morphology), and their interrelation in sentences (syntax). Grammar focuses on punctuation; structure (or syntax) and vocabulary. Language is the basic means used by human beings to communicate with one another.

God has chosen to communicate with humanity through a special love language. Indeed, God uses the **grammar of grace**.

I.   The Punctuation of a Deadly Plight (verses 1 – 3)

II. The Structure of a Dynamic Salvation (verses 4 – 9)

– 79 –

Captive Christianity

Ephesians 4: 1 [1-13] (KJV)

[1] I therefore, the prisoner of the Lord, beseech you
that ye walk worthy of the vocation wherewith ye are called,

The first three chapters of Ephesians address our *wealth in Christ* while the last three focus on our *walk in Christ*. This passage is transitional. After presenting doctrinal content in the first three chapters, the Apostle Paul with a pastor's heart links the teaching to the times in Chapters 4-6 with practical applications of the doctrines he just expounded. His repeated emphasis on a believer's "walk" is the unique signature of this section. The New International Version translates "walk" as "live."

This passage constitutes a virtual prison tour. The Apostle Paul acknowledges here that he was living in the Lord's lockup. He was a man under constraint. His ministry was transacted in a spiritual lockdown. He once said, "For though I preach the gospel, I have nothing to glory of: for necessity is laid upon me; yea, woe is unto me, if I preach not the gospel! (1 Corinthians 9:16 - KJV)

I.   A Perspective We Must Acknowledge (verse 1)

    a.   Paul's language in this text is laced with the vernacular and nomenclature of incarceration, captivity and confinement.

II.   A Pattern We Must Adopt (verses 2 – 6)

    a.   The evidence of Christian character

    b.   The experience of Christian community

III. A Provision We Must Appropriate (verses 7 -12)

IV.   A Promise We Must Anticipate (verse 13)

"Oh joy that seekest me through pain
I cannot close my heart to thee
I climb the rainbow in the rain and feel the promise is not vain;
that morn shall tearless be!" (George Matheson)

– 80 –

Dressed to Kill

Ephesians 6:10-11 [1-11] (KJV)

[10] **Finally, my brethren, be strong in the Lord, and in the power of his might.** [11] **Put on the whole armour of God, that ye may be able to stand against the wiles of the devil.**

No image of the Christian life is more compelling than that of the Christian soldier. I remember learning the words of a song as a little boy that said, "We are soldiers in the army, we have to fight although we have to cry. We have to hold up the blood stained banner, we have to hold it up until we die."

In the period A.D. 60-62, the Apostle Paul, was imprisoned in Rome. Perhaps observing from some corner or crevice of his prison cell a Roman soldier standing sentry in full regalia, he was inspired to write these words. He creatively wheels and weaves this military and combat metaphor into a message designed to challenge the saints at Ephesus. Like them, we are in a fight like no other! So it is important to suit up when facing our old Enemy and dress to kill.

I.   Embrace the Privileges of the Precedent (verse 10)

II.   Enjoy the Prerogatives of the Position (verse 11)

III. Experience the Pervasiveness of the Power (verses 12 – 17)

IV.   Engage the Potency of the Provision (verse 18)

The God Who Stooped So We Can Stand
(An Advent Message)

Philippians 2:5-8 [1-11] (NIV)

[5] **Your attitude should be the same as that of Christ Jesus:**
[6] **Who, being in very nature God, did not consider equality with God something to be grasped,** [7] **but made himself nothing, taking the very nature of a servant, being made in human likeness.** [8] **And being found in appearance as a man, he humbled himself and became obedient to death-- even death on a cross!**

The Apostle Paul's pastoral heart is on full blast in this passage. His encouragement and exhortation is based on the ultimate Exemplar of true Christian humility and heroism. The dictionary defines "stoop" as "the lowering of oneself; to bend forward; to descend or condescend; to be humble or subject." Paul uses the example of Jesus, "the mind [or attitude] of Christ" to encourage unity amidst discord in the church. The essential message then and now is "mimic the mind and model of Jesus" who stooped so we could stand!

I. God Stooped in the Majesty of His Heavenly Relationships (verses 5 – 6)

II. God Stooped in the Mystery of His Human Revelation (verses 7 – 8)

III. God Stooped in the Ministry of His Humiliating Redemption (verses 9 – 11)

> "O come, all ye faithful,
> Joyful and triumphant,
> Come ye, O come ye to Bethlehem;
> Come and behold Him,
> Born the King of angels;
> O come, let us adore Him,
> O come, let us adore Him,
> O come, let us adore Him,
> Christ, the Lord." (18th century hymn)

Living Life on a Need to Know Basis

Philippians 3:10-11 [4-14] (KJV)

¹⁰ That I may know him, and the power of his resurrection,
and the fellowship of his sufferings,
being made conformable unto his death; ¹¹ If by any means
I might attain unto the resurrection of the dead.

If you share with someone on "a need-to-know basis," you only tell them the facts they need to know at the time they need to know them, and nothing more. The Apostle Paul displays a remarkable reductionism in this text. When he factored his life down to the lowest common denominator ("highest common factor" – British) by dividing the essence of his being by the experience of his belief, the most fundamental value and variable was the knowledge of Christ. Twice in this paragraph in Philippians he refers to the pursuit of this prize which was his magnificent obsession.

I.   Know the <u>Person</u> of Christ (*"That I may know him"*)

II. Know the <u>Power</u> of Christ (*"and the power of his resurrection"*)

III. Know the <u>Passion</u> of Christ (*"and the fellowship of his sufferings"*)

IV. Know the <u>Promises</u> of Christ (*"being made conformable unto his death; If by any means I might attain unto the resurrection of the dead"*)

"I got a robe,
You got a robe,
All God's children got robes.
When we get to heaven
We're going to put on our robes
We're going to shut all over God's heaven." (Negro Spiritual)

Overcoming the Pull of the Past

Philippians 3:13-14 (NIV)

[13] Brothers, I do not consider myself yet to have taken hold of it. But one thing I do: Forgetting what is behind and straining toward what is ahead, [14] I press on toward the goal to win the prize for which God has called me heavenward in Christ Jesus.

In this chapter of one of Paul's most buoyant and joyful letters; albeit written from prison, the noted apostle is occupied with Christ; Jesus Christ and Him crucified was Paul's MAGNIFICENT OBSESSION (and should be ours). When you read Paul's writings in the New Testament, you get the sense that he was haunted by his sins and transgressions particularly the persecution of the church which he did "ignorantly and in unbelief" (1 Timothy 1:13). His faults, frailties and failures always seemed to appear in the rearview mirror of his consciousness. He recognizes that his pursuit of excellence could be jeopardized by the "pull of the past." Some things must be jettisoned; there are items that we carry on the flight of the Christian life that should be checked at the gate.

I.   Practice a Holy Discontent in the Present (verse 13a)

II.   Promote a Healthy Detachment from the Past (verse 13b)

III. Pursue a Heavenly Destiny in the Future (verse 14)

    a.   "The only way to dispossess the heart of an old affection is by the expulsive power of a new affection. We know of no other way by which to keep the love of the world out of our hearts than to keep in our hearts the love of God." Scottish preacher – Thomas Chalmers [1780-1847]

A Leader Who Lasted

2 Timothy 1:11-12 [6-14] (KJV)

[11] Whereunto I am appointed a preacher, and an apostle, and a teacher of the Gentiles. [12] For the which cause I also suffer these things: nevertheless I am not ashamed: for I know whom I have believed, and am persuaded that he is able to keep that which I have committed unto him against that day.

Paul, a leader who lasted unveils his heart as he writes words of encouragement to his son in the ministry. In this compellingly timeless text we have the magnificent musings of a mature minister, the wonderful witness of a wise warrior, the solemn sentiments of a seasoned servant, and the dynamic declarations of a devoted disciple. The sacred record of this book is that he lasted; that he finished his course. The question emerges, "How did he last?" In the same way you and I can last if we recognize that the Christian race is not a fifty-yard dash but a marathon.

I. He Was Engaged by a Supernatural Calling (verse 11)

II. He Was Exercised by a Sanctifying Conflict (verse 12a)

III. He Was Encouraged by a Satisfying Connection (verse 12b)

IV. He Was Emboldened by a Stabilizing Confidence (verse 12c)

What Every Christian Needs to Know

2 Timothy 1:11-12 (NIV)

[11] And of this gospel I was appointed a herald and an apostle and a teacher. [12] That is why I am suffering as I am. Yet I am not ashamed, because I know whom I have believed, and am convinced that he is able to guard what I have entrusted to him for that day.

Our knowledge of essential biblical and spiritual information is often like the four-year old who responded to her teacher's question in Sunday School Class on Palm Sunday. The teacher asked the class, "Do you know what today is?" The little girl said, "It is Palm Sunday." Commending the little girl, the teacher then asked the class, "What is next Sunday?" The same little girl raised her hand and said, "Next Sunday is Easter Sunday." The teacher once again applauded the little girl for her knowledge and then asked the class, "Now does anyone know what makes next Sunday Easter?" The same little girl responded, "Yes, next Sunday is Easter because Jesus rose from the dead!" Before the teacher could congratulate her once again, the little girl added, "But if He sees His shadow, he has to go back in for seven weeks!"

According to this passage and particularly verse 12, there are three things every Christian needs to know. Do you want to know what they are?

I.   We Need to Know the Person of God (*"because I know whom I have believed"*)

II.   We Need to Know the Power of God (*"and am convinced that he is able to guard"*)

III. We Need to Know the Plan of God (*"what I have entrusted to him for that day"*)

– 86 –

A Winner's View of Victory

2 Timothy 4:6-8 [1-8] (KJV)

⁶ For I am now ready to be offered, and the time of my departure is at hand. ⁷ I have fought a good fight, I have finished *my* course, I have kept the faith:
⁸ Henceforth there is laid up for me a crown of righteousness, which the Lord, the righteous judge,
shall give me at that day: and not to me only,
but unto all them also that love his appearing.

The Apostle Paul died a winner because he did not live like a loser. Even while in prison and expecting to be executed, he had a winner's view or vantage point of victory. He shares this perspective with Timothy, his son in the ministry. Like Timothy, we can be encouraged by his words and live out his example because every child of God has been set apart to be a winner in the devil's world.

I.   Life is A Fight - Don't Give Up! (*"I have fought a good fight"*)

II. Life is A Race – Don't Give Out! (*"I have finished my course"*)

III. Life is A Trust – Don't Give In! (*"I have kept the faith"*)

– 87 –

The Exceptional Exception

2 Timothy 4:16-18 (KJV)

[16] **At my first answer no man stood with me, but all** *men* **forsook me:** *I pray God* **that it may not be laid to their charge.** [17] **Notwithstanding the Lord stood with me, and strengthened me; that by me the preaching might be fully known, and** *that* **all the Gentiles might hear: and I was delivered out of the mouth of the lion.** [18] **And the Lord shall deliver me from every evil work, and will preserve** *me* **unto his heavenly kingdom: to whom** *be* **glory for ever and ever. Amen.**

There are points and places in our spiritual journeys where the Lord places a conjunction where life has placed a period. This experience for the Apostle Paul, estranged from many who loved and supported his ministry was the context and background from which he acknowledged in this text that God is present when all else fails and when we are left alone. God is *"the Exceptional Exception."*

I.   God Stayed With Him (verse 16)

    a.   When others forsook him

II. God Stood With Him (verse 17)

    a. When others forgot him

III. God Struggled With Him (verse 18)

    a. When others failed him

    b. Paul's mission was not stymied, stopped or stalled because of his imprisonment. Rather in the third instance, God was in the struggle and straits with him advancing the Gospel and the Kingdom of God. Even in prison and facing trial and execution, he was in the will of God.

– 88 –

The Day Grace Appeared
(An Advent Message)

Titus 2:11-14 (NIV)

[11] For the grace of God that brings salvation has appeared to all men. [12] It teaches us to say "No" to ungodliness and worldly passions, and to live self-controlled, upright and godly lives in this present age, [13] while we wait for the blessed hope--the glorious appearing of our great God and Savior, Jesus Christ, [14] who gave himself for us to redeem us from all wickedness and to purify for himself a people that are his very own, eager to do what is good.

Christmas according to the Apostle Paul in this passage is a "grace appearing." Twice he uses the word "appearing" in this passage – it translates the word in the original from which we derive our English word *epiphany*. The word describes the appearance or manifestation of deity. Outside of this passage, the word occurs only twice in the New Testament – In Zacharias's prayer (the Benedictus) recorded in Luke 1:79 – "give light to them that sit in darkness" and in Acts 27:20 where it refers to the illumination of heavenly bodies – the stars and planets. Whatever else Christmas is, it is THE DAY THAT GRACE APPEARED. Christmas is the Epiphany of Grace.

I.   Grace Saves Us (verses 11, 14a)

II.   Grace Sanctifies Us (verses 12, 14b)

III. Grace Stabilizes Us (verse 13)

> *"God is present with me in the midst of my anxieties. I affirm in my own heart and the mind the reality of His presence. He makes immediately available to me the strength of His goodness, the reassurance of His wisdom and the heartiness of His courage."* (Howard Thurman, Meditations of the Heart)

– 89 –

The Faith That Overcomes Our Fears

Hebrews 4:12 [12-16] (KJV)

¹² For the word of God *is* quick, and powerful, and sharper than any twoedged sword, piercing even to the dividing asunder of soul and spirit, and of the joints and marrow, and *is* a discerner of the thoughts and intents of the heart.

The Word of God is a sword; not just any sword but a double-edged sword (Greek MACHAIRA – revolutionized ancient warfare; compactness; efficiency as a weapon). There was an old Mother at my former church who was fond of saying – when a preacher authentically preaches the word of God; he leaves the pulpit "as bloody as a butcher." "Two-edged" means that the instrument cuts coming and going which is why we don't preach at people but preach to people. The Word of God saves, sanctifies and sustains.

I.   It is Anchored by the Powerful Word of the Spirit (verses 12, 13)

II.   It is Assisted by the Priestly Work of the Savior (verses 14, 15)

III. It is Activated by the Perfect Weapon of the Saved (verse 16)

The Heavenly Cure for Earthly Care
(An Easter Message)
Hebrews 4:14-16 (KJV)

[14] Seeing then that we have a great high priest, that is passed into the heavens, Jesus the Son of God, let us hold fast *our* profession. [15] For we have not an high priest which cannot be touched with the feeling of our infirmities; but was in all points tempted like as *we are, yet* without sin. [16] Let us therefore come boldly unto the throne of grace, that we may obtain mercy, and find grace to help in time of need.

Imagine the headlines in the newspapers if a cure was found for cancer; high blood pressure, Alzheimer's or diabetes. Television and the internet would be saturated with the details of these epic, life-changing discoveries. There is something far better in this text – the heavenly cure for earthly care. In the context of this chapter of the Book of Hebrews, this cure is the foundation for the rest [not chronological or covenantal but relational] we experience in the Christian life. We rest, repose, relax and recline in the sufficiency of the Savior who is simply BETTER than anything the world can offer. This relational rest has no precedent or peer.

I. The Position He Occupies Strengthens Our Faith (verse 14)

II. The Perfection He Obtains Secures Our Salvation (verse 15)

III. The Provision He Offers Satisfies Our Need (verse 16)

Paid in Full

Hebrews 10:11-14 (KJV)

[11] And every priest standeth daily ministering and offering oftentimes the same sacrifices, which can never take away sins: [12] But this man, after he had offered one sacrifice for sins for ever, sat down on the right hand of God; [13] From henceforth expecting till his enemies be made his footstool. [14] For by one offering he hath perfected forever them that are sanctified.

There is no sweeter sight to the eyes or sweeter sound to the ears of someone who owes a large debt than the words, "paid in full." This text and its larger context constitute a kind of *spiritual receipt* for the ages. The hymn writer captures the essence of this fundamental affirmation of our faith with the words,

> *"I hear the Savior say, "Thy strength in-deed is small!*
> *Child of weakness, watch and pray,*
> *Find in me thine all in all."*
> *Jesus paid it all, All to Him I owe; Sin has left a crimson*
> *stain – He washed it white as snow."* (Elvina M. Hall)

I.   Paid in Full with a Lasting Sacrifice
     (verse 11 - *Source of our Peace*)

II. Paid in Full with a Living Sacrifice
     (verse 12 - *Source of our Purpose*)

III. Paid in Full with a Liberating Sacrifice
     (verse 13 - *Source of our Power*)

> *"Jesus paid it all,*
> *All to Him I owe,*
> *Sin has left a crimson stain,*
> *He washed it white as snow."*

– 92 –

Finding Treasure in God's Pleasure

Hebrews 11:6 (KJV)

 [6] But without faith *it is* impossible to please *him*: for he that cometh to God must believe that he is, and *that* he is a rewarder of them that diligently seek him.

Those who received this letter were in danger of forsaking their faith, returning to Judaism and missing out on life's greatest treasure - experiencing the pleasure and favor of God as it is ultimately revealed in the life of His Son and our Savior Jesus Christ. In contrast Enoch, that great antediluvian saint is lifted up in this chapter as an exemplary model whose faith led him to experience fellowship and intimacy with God that had no rival in his evil and wicked generation. An exploration of the text reveals three principles or priorities necessary for finding treasure in God's pleasure.

I.   Exercising the Requirement That Has No Exception (verse 6a)

II. Experiencing the Relationship That Has No Equal (verse 6b)

III. Enjoying the Reward That Has No Expiration (verse 6c)

– 93 –

In It to Win It!

Hebrews 12:1-2 (KJV)

[1] Wherefore seeing we also are compassed about with so great a cloud of witnesses, let us lay aside every weight, and the sin which doth so easily beset *us*, and let us run with patience the race that is set before us, [2] Looking unto Jesus the author and finisher of *our* faith; who for the joy that was set before him endured the cross, despising the shame, and is set down at the right hand of the throne of God.

With a pastor's heart, the author seeks to encourage and strengthen the faith of God's people. He likens their situation [and ours] to that of Olympic runners who have entered the arena amidst the hoopla and applause of thousands of spectators and reminds them again and again that they are "in it to win it." It is true; the arena of life is filled with heartbreak, sickness, sorrow, pressure, stress, hardship and even death. Yes, it is true that demonic forces have been unleashed whose primary objective is to undermine our faith in God and to "steal, kill and destroy." But it is also true that God has assured us of victory and every Christian who runs this race of faith should be IN IT TO WIN IT.

I.   Listen Up

II. Lighten Up

III. Lace Up

IV. Look Up

– 94 –

A Calculated Joy

James 1:2-6 [1-12] (KJV)

[2] My brethren, count it all joy when ye fall into divers temptations; [3] Knowing this, that the trying of your faith worketh patience. [4] But let patience have her perfect work, that ye may be perfect and entire, wanting nothing. [5] If any of you lack wisdom, let him ask of God, that giveth to all men liberally, and upbraideth not; and it shall be given him. [6] But let him ask in faith, nothing wavering. For he that wavereth is like a wave of the sea driven with the wind and tossed.

James, the Lord's brother and acknowledged leader in the early church is the ultimate Christian practitioner. While the book that bears his name has been the object of canonical controversy, he addresses concretely the testing that will inevitably come in the believer's life. In every life, there will at some point be pressures without and doubts within. Yet our happiness does not depend on "happenings" but rather on the irreplaceable joy that is part and parcel of our relationship with Jesus Christ. That joy is calculated and calibrated to meet our needs.

I.   How to Receive

II. How to Perceive

III. How to Achieve

IV. How to Relieve

V.   How to Believe

– 95 –

Advancing in Adversity

James 1:2-4 (NIV)

² Consider it pure joy, my brothers, whenever you face trials of many kinds, ³ because you know that the testing of your faith develops perseverance. ⁴ Perseverance must finish its work so that you may be mature and complete, not lacking anything.

Bible teacher, pastor and noted author Chuck Swindoll wrote that "much of life's music is played in the minor key. Hurts, headaches, pain, problems, disappointment, sickness, suffering, disease, and death pile up on us and *won't go away.*" He is right in his analysis. There is a persistent heaviness that characterizes our lives. It lingers and will not be relieved and released by money, success, fame or power.

Furthermore, the child of God is not exempted or excluded from this phenomenon. It is not flippant or fanciful to say, "In every life a little rain must fall." This is factual and is much like the warning on the back of the trash truck that said, "*This truck makes frequent stops.*" While we would like to move down the freeways of life without pause or peril, the reality is that all of us must stop at some time. Adversity – trouble, trials and tribulations stops us or slows us down. How do we advance in these circumstances?

I.   Adversity Encourages Our Joy ("*Consider it pure joy*")

II.   Adversity Enhances Our Faith (*"the testing of your faith"*)

III. Adversity Enables Our Growth (*"so that you may be mature"*)

– 96 –

The Message in the Mist
(Facing the Certainty of Uncertainty)

James 4:14 (NIV)

14 Why, you do not even know what will happen tomorrow. What is your life? You are a mist that appears for a little while and then vanishes.

Life is an enigma. It is fleeting, illusive, numinous, transitory and uncertain. Preachers, poets and philosophers have grappled with this reality. One said, "Life is a hollow bubble vulnerable to the prick of any pin" (E. B. Cooke). Another noted, "Life is a tale told by an idiot, full of sound and fury signifying nothing" (William Shakespeare).

How do we face the uncertainty that is a <u>certain</u> and inescapable characteristic of our lives from day to day? This text provides a clue.

I.   The Fallacy that Hurts Us

II.   The Frailty that Haunts Us

III. The Faith that Helps Us

> *"I've got to walk my lonesome valley,*
> *I've got to walk it for myself.*
> *Nobody else can walk it for me,*
> *I've got to walk it for myself!"* (Negro Spiritual)

A Ready Witness

1 Peter 3:15 (KJV)

[15] But sanctify the Lord God in your hearts: and be ready always to give an answer to every man that asketh you a reason of the hope that is in you with meekness and fear:

A fundamental part of being a child of God is witnessing. We are God's witnesses to a dying world; to a world that is no friend of grace. We are called to be witnesses in our homes, schools, community, jobs and even at churches where we are members and serve. No scripture captures the essence of this responsibility more clearly than the one before us.

I find it refreshing and encouraging that the words of our text were penned by a man who at a point in time failed miserably as a witness. When Jesus was on trial, Peter denied that he even knew Him. Jesus is on trial in our world today. The Apostle Peter provides in this passage a profile of a "ready witness." A ready witness is just that, *ready* to share the truth about Jesus Christ whenever an opportunity is available. A ready witness is not shy or reserved but invites the opportunity to share his or her faith with someone else. Like Paul and Silas in prison, a ready witness responds to someone who asks, "What must I do to be saved," with "I'm glad you asked."

I.   A Ready Witness Is Passionate

II.   A Ready Witness is Prepared

III. A Ready Witness is Positive

The Best is Yet to Come

1 John 3:1-3 (KJV)

[1] Behold, what manner of love the Father hath bestowed upon us, that we should be called the sons of God: therefore the world knoweth us not, because it knew him not. [2] Beloved, now are we the sons of God, and it doth not yet appear what we shall be: but we know that, when he shall appear, we shall be like him; for we shall see him as he is. [3] And every man that hath this hope in him purifieth himself, even as he is pure.

Our lives often resemble a roller coast ride with its peaks and valleys; ups and downs; its highs and lows. Whatever our struggle though, the essence of what it truly means to be a Christian is to live our lives with the faith that the best is yet to come. John the aged Apostle wrote to people who were discouraged either by their own failures or the failures of those around them. His purpose was to encourage them that God had not left them alone; that God was faithful and was still at work in their lives.

I. There is a Provision that Enriches Us (verse 1a)

II. There is a Pedigree that Enables Us (verse 1b)

III. There is a Process that Engages Us (verse 2a)

IV. There is a Prospect that Encourages Us (verses 2b – 3)

> *"Oh, He's going to wake up the dead,*
> *Going to wake up the dead,*
> *God's going to wake up the dead.*
> *One of these mornings bright and fair,*
> *God's going to wake up the dead."* (Negro Spiritual)

– 99 –

The Biography of a Contender

Jude 1:3 (KJV)

³ Beloved, when I gave all diligence to write unto you of the common salvation, it was needful for me to write unto you, and exhort you that ye should earnestly contend for the faith which was once delivered unto the saints.

The word translated "contends" in our text translates a word in the original language from which we get our English word "agony." It means here to "agonize earnestly" with all diligence in defense of those truths, which ungodly men were trying to destroy. The first sixteen verses of this book answer the question, "Why contend?" The last eighteen verses answer the question "How to contend?" Nestled neatly at the precipice of this summons to service and sacrifice is our verse. This very familiar passage constitutes a "call to arms" for every Christian soldier and for the church today.

I.   The Fellowship of the Contender

II. The Focus of the Contender

III. The Faith of the Contender

IV. The Finish and Future of the Contender

– 100 –

The Kind of Church the Lord Blesses

Revelation 2:10 [8-11] (KJV)

¹⁰ Fear none of those things which thou shalt suffer: behold, the devil shall cast some of you into prison, that ye may be tried; and ye shall have tribulation ten days: be thou faithful unto death, and I will give thee a crown of life.

While reading and reflecting on this text, I thought about the story of the young, bright and promising college student who received the grade of "F" for a paper she wrote for her college

English class. When she asked her professor about it, the professor said that while the paper was clear, concise, compelling and comprehensive, he could not award her a passing grade because she failed to address the assigned topic. What would Jesus say if he stood in the midst of our churches today and evaluated our ministry? Are we addressing the assigned topic?

The commendation that the church of Smyrna receives in this passage and its larger context provides clear clues about the kind of church, or for that matter, the kind of Christian that the LORD blesses.

I.   An Uncompromising Church (*"Be thou faithful"*)

II.   An Unflagging Church (*"unto death"*)

III. An Unconquerable Church (*"and I will give thee a crown of life"*)